Praise for

faith & favor: Discovering Family at Fifty

"I was impressed by Li's storytelling capabilities. She included photos, text conversations, and messages between family members throughout her discovery. Li's faith and trust in timing is inspiring."

—CARA GARRISON

"The story was a compelling and easy read. I stayed up until the wee hours of the morning to finish it. The strength and determination that Lisa exhibited will aid others on their own journey."

—DEE VAUGHN

"This book made me smile and shed a tear more than once. This is a must read for adoptees seeking their roots but also for those who aren't but would like to know how it feels to have those questions."

—GORDON SUDBECK

"Lisa takes you on a fascinating journey to find her roots. You will ride the crest during the highs and suffer through the lows with her. I could not put this page-turner down."

—ALLAN NODDLE

"This book paints a beautiful picture of patience, endurance, love, joy, hope and happiness."

—E GAYLE HAMILTON CRUSE

faith & favor

DISCOVERING FAMILY AT FIFTY

LISA A. QUAITES

Omaha, Nebraska

Lisa A. Quaites/Summer Solstice Publishing LLC

PO Box 34342

Omaha, NE 68134

www.summersolsticepublishing.com

Cover design by Cara Garrison Graphic Design

Book Layout © 2020 BookDesignTemplates.com

Editorial services by Elizabeth Sheridan and Mary Anne Shepard

All images are from the author's personal collection.

Author photo by Capris Quaites

Ordering Information:

Quantity sales. Special discounts are available on quantity purchases by corporations, associations, and others. For details, contact the "Special Sales Department" at the address above.

Faith & Favor/Lisa A. Quaites—1st ed.

ISBN 978-1-7358201-0-1

Dedicated to my three mothers. Chung Suk-ah who gave me life, Mildred who taught me how to live, and Beatrice, who mentored me through it. To say I love you is not enough.

ACKNOWLEDGEMENTS

So many people helped bring this story to life, but I must first thank God for trusting me with this testimony. Sandra Wendel, I appreciate your coaching, guidance, and references. Thank you for caring about my story. Omaha Night Writers, I don't know what I would have done without your critiques. You are a gifted group of authors who taught me the craft. A huge thank you to my beta readers. Your feedback helped shape this narrative for a wider audience. To my Korean adoptee community, I hear your stories and I'm inspired by your resilience. To the family I was born in to, and to the family that raised me, my love for you is immeasurable. To my beautiful daughters, thank you for your honest opinions and for serving as my consultants. You are God's most precious gifts to me. And to my husband James. Thank you for showing me what real-world unconditional love looks like and how it works. I love you today.

Contents

CHAPTER 1

Searching for Answers

MY ADOPTION HAD NEVER been a secret to me or anyone in my adoptive family, but it was not something that I spoke of often. It was a part of me that I accepted but kept tucked away. Periodically, fleeting thoughts about my birth mother danced back and forth in the random depths of my mind. What did she look like? Did I look like her? Was she nice? Did she ever think about me or wonder where I was or how I was doing? Did she ever regret giving me up? Where was she? How old was she? Was she still alive? What was her name? I had so many questions that I just accepted would go unanswered.

Although I am Black and Korean, I knew nothing about Korean culture. The Midwestern version of Korean food did not top my list of favorite cuisines. I had no burning desire to learn about my homeland or any of its customs. I didn't know that Korean culture camps existed for kids. My adoptive parents didn't expose me to anything Korean, therefore I never connected with the country of my birth.

I was raised by a Black family who told me I was Black, because to them, anyone with even a small percentage of Black ancestry was considered Black. It felt natural and comfortable for me to identify with the culture of my adoptive family.

Fast forward to adulthood. A deep-seated longing to connect with my birth mother surfaced during my late forties. Why then? Why wait until I was middle-aged? Then again, why not while I was middle-aged? My children were at an age where they were independent and self-sufficient, leaving more time for me to focus on myself. Neither I nor my birth mother were getting any younger. I prayed that she was still alive and well. I prayed that I would one day get to hug her and let her know how much I appreciated her sacrifice, and how much I loved her. I wanted her to know that I turned out ok.

The desire to connect with blood relatives and know about inherited health conditions is a normal human aspiration.

Searching for one's biological family is immensely personal. Many emotions surface. Fear of the unknown. Guilt. Betrayal. Frustration. Disappointment. Flip the coin, and elation, excitement, and love can accompany acceptance when estranged families reunite.

In March 2015, I started a formal birth family search through the agency in my adoptive country. United States-based Holt International responded with disappointing news. They could not verify that their children's services department had facilitated my adoption. They recommended I contact Holt Korea, a separate organization. I acted upon Holt's suggestion, but repeated emails to their birth family search representative went unanswered. There's nothing like being stuck on step one of a multistep process.

Not willing to give up, I reviewed the paperwork given to my parents when my adoption was finalized, hoping those documents would be a starting point for my search and lend clues to my mother's past. The rice paper pages had Korean words written on them, with English translations on separate sheets. I assumed the Asian characters were Hangul, the Korean alphabet, although older legal documents were printed in Chinese due to the ambiguous nature of the Korean language. Hangul is phonetic, therefore two distinct words with the same sounds would be spelled the same. Printing those words in Chinese adds clarity to the meaning.

The packet of papers was bound together in the upper left-hand corner by a half-inch flat metal ring that sat flush against the pages, like a staple. A red ribbon, laced through the ring, ran vertically down the left-hand side of the top page. The Great Seal of the United States, in a matching shade of candy apple red, secured the ribbon near the bottom of the page. Among the various forms, the official certificate of adoption was legally binding in Korea and recognized by US law.

A few of the forms had my permanent and present address listed as #382-14 Hap Jung-Dong, Ma Po Ku, Seoul. All children adopted through Holt Korea likely had the same address on their adoption paperwork. It matched the Holt Korea office, and did not offer any clues as to where an adoptee's birth family might have resided at the time.

The most misleading form in the packet was the Ho Juk Deung Bon (family registration). It was full of what appeared to be useful information, but in reality, the contents would likely lead adoptees to search for their roots down the wrong rabbit hole.

The Korean family register lists all births, deaths, and marriages within a male lineage, with the oldest living male designated as the family chief. Recorded on the register are all the males in the family, along with their wives. Daughters are listed on their father's register until they marry, at which time their registration is transferred to their husband's family register. Korean incest laws traditionally prevented citizens with the same surname from marrying, so family origin played a huge role in determining relations.

This Korean equivalent to a US birth certificate listed my mother and father as unknown. Prior to 2012, a child was not eligible for adoption if they appeared on their father's family register. The catch-22 was that, in order for a child to be adopted, they were required to have a family register. To rectify that dilemma, the Korean government created a family register for each orphan and listed the child as family chief, with a randomly assigned family origin.

Unfortunately, for those of us searching for answers, that bogus information had no value when trying to figure out where our ancestors came from. How disappointed I was to learn that the permanent address, family chief information, lack of record of mother or father, family origin, guardian name, and address had nothing to do with me personally. It made me question whether my birth name was Lee, Augustine, as listed in the paperwork. What Korean woman names her daughter Augustine? It doesn't follow the normal name format of three syllables, consisting of one surname and two personal names: Lee, Ok Soon, for example. Both personal names are considered first names, and no middle name is used. The surname comes before the personal name, signifying the importance of family over individuals.

Separate from the bound packet were multiple medical reports and an x-ray of my two-year-old chest. The most extensive medical exam was dated August 9, 1969, a significant date for me. That was Beatrice's (my late mother-in-law) birth month and day. It was also the day before my second birthday.

The thorough medical exam and x-ray were performed at Bo Yook Hospital and signed by a visa medical examiner. The medical report looked to be a standardized form, filled in with handwritten responses and annotations. The report was detailed enough to list how many teeth I had (10/10) but did not specify my height or weight.

A separate Medical Examination of Visa Applicants stated that I had recovered from a measles epidemic at the orphanage, but otherwise had no defect, disease, or disability. It also listed immunizations that I had been given.

A pre-flight child report gave a concise picture of two-year-old Augustine Lee. This was my last physical exam prior to boarding a plane destined for my new home. According to the report, I was reluctant to eat and didn't like green onions, a trait that would follow me throughout life. I fed myself but didn't get dressed without assistance. I slept heavily and was well toilet-trained. I spoke clearly and sang well with correct melody and tune. The report declared I was alert, happy, and played actively with the other children, without being greedy with toys. They evaluated me to be sociable with the understanding of a four- or five-year-old, although I was only two. I was friendly to adults, affectionate, and loved cuddles.

The insight I gained from the barely legible typewritten words on that translucent paper revealed that my preferences and tendencies had withstood the test of time. Not much had changed with me since I was a toddler, except assistance to get dressed was no longer needed.

I was not in the orphanage for very long. Admitted on July 11, 1969, my adoption was finalized by October 31, 1969. Before reading my paperwork, I mistakenly thought I had been in an orphanage since birth and remained there until I was adopted at two years of age.

It wasn't much to go on, but I had started my birth family search and was committed to diving even deeper.

CHAPTER 2

Three DNA Tests

I'D OFTEN FANTASIZED ABOUT what my birth parents looked like. I envisioned my mother's fair Asian skin and her straight black hair. I figured my father's complexion was a darker hue, since my time in the sun produced a deep caramel glow. I wondered what else I inherited from them. I had no eyelashes, small boobs, and gigantic calves. Whose features were those?

The popularity of consumer genealogy testing was on the rise and I had seen advertisements on different media platforms. December was a good month to order the tests online because deep discounts enticed holiday shoppers to buy tests for themselves and for loved ones as gifts.

In December 2017, I received the three DNA collection kits that I ordered online. I laid each box down on the bathroom counter. I read the instructions for each kit and started with 23andMe.

"What are you doing?" my husband asked as he appeared in the doorway. It's no fair how good men look in the morning with no effort at all. His tall and lean 6'2" build hadn't changed a whole lot since his college football days. Amazing for a fifty-three-year-old man.

I greeted him with a smile. "I saw this segment on TV a few weeks ago, and they were talking about DNA tests. They had triplets take three different tests and they shared the results."

"Oh yeah, I saw that," James said.

"The triplets each took three tests, from Ancestry, 23andMe, and MyHeritage. Each test identified them as siblings, and according to their report, the results were accurate." I put the instructions on the counter.

"Hmmm…" James lifted his chin.

"So I was thinking…"

"What were you thinking, baby?"

I smirked at his playful response. "Well, I was thinking that I don't know my family health history and it would also be nice to know my ethnic makeup."

James nodded his head in agreement.

"My parents always told me my biological father was an African American serviceman and my mother was South Korean. It'd be nice to know for sure."

"Yep. So why are you doing three tests?"

"Just to see how accurate they are and if the data matches. I ordered the same tests that were featured on *Good Morning America,* so they seem legit. I paid extra for 23andMe because they provide health history reports that let you know if your DNA indicates you are susceptible to Alzheimer's or Parkinson's and stuff like that."

James shifted his weight in the doorway and said, "Well, I hope it works for you, honey."

"Thank you." I smiled as I looked into his brown eyes. He stepped into the bathroom and caressed my long salt-and-pepper hair, then tilted my chin up. He planted a slobbery kiss on my unsuspecting lips.

"Hey!" I exclaimed once my lips escaped his. "Don't mix your DNA with mine!"

"You're gonna have more Black in you than you thought!" He chuckled as he made a sharp turn to exit the bathroom.

"Heeeyy!" I shouted after him while wiping his saliva off my mouth. His heavy footsteps were joined by the pitter-patter of doggie paws as the males of the household retreated down the hallway.

I refocused on the task at hand. The white box with images of colored chromosomes on the package was the first target. A green "Hi, Let's Get Started!" guide greeted me as I peered into the box. I read through the instructions and went to grab my laptop out of my backpack in the entryway closet. When I returned to my bathroom, I cleared off some space on the pearl-gray quartz countertop to make room for my computer. I went to 23andMe.com and clicked Register Kit from the home page. That gave me the opportunity to create an account and link it to the fourteen-digit barcode from the collection tube in my kit. Once my online registration was complete, I removed the saliva collection tube from the plastic insert and attached the funnel lid as per the instructions. I mustered up enough saliva to fill the vial to the fill line. It grossed me out, even though it was my own spit. I sealed the tube as instructed and shook it to allow the DNA stabilization buffer solution to mix with my sample. I inserted the sealed tube into the specimen bag and returned it to the original box.

One test down, two to go. The process for Ancestry was similar to 23andMe. MyHeritage opted for a buccal swab as the method of DNA collection, which I welcomed since my saliva well had run dry. The kit had two cotton swabs, two vials of liquid, and an envelope addressed to the MyHeritage lab. I activated the kit online per the instructions. I used one cotton swab and rubbed it on the inside of my cheek for sixty seconds, then placed it in one of the liquid-filled vials. I broke the stick off of the cotton swab, then closed and sealed the little tube. I repeated that process with the second swab and other cheek. When finished, I placed both samples in the provided envelope and said a prayer to ask God to bless the results of all the tests.

My youngest daughter, Candace, called me via FaceTime. Whenever I spoke directly to her, I called her by her middle name. "Hey, Simonie!"

"Liza!" Over the years, she always came up with different nicknames for me, but that one had stuck the longest. "What are you doing?"

"I ordered some DNA tests and just got done getting the samples together."

"Oh, that's cool. What'd you have to do?"

"Spit in these little vials. I shouldn't have done three at the same time. I ran out of saliva! Not sure how they expect you to produce that much spit when you are dehydrated!"

"Why are you dehydrated?"

"Because the instructions say you can't eat or drink anything for at least thirty minutes prior to collecting the samples."

"Liza…" Candace shook her head at me. "Well, not to change the subject, but my birthday is coming up!"

"Yes, honey, I know, December 22 is right around the corner. What are your plans?"

She paused for a split second. "I take my last final on December 21. It's my O Chem final, and Mom, I'm stressing!"

"Honey, you know it's going to be hard. You just need to make sure you are as prepared as possible."

"I know, Mom. I've been going in for extra help, and my friends and I have been studying together. It's just a lot of information and I need to do well on this exam."

"If it were easy then everyone would be doing it, and it wouldn't mean as much. The harder you work to grasp something, the better it feels when you hold it in your hands."

"I know, Mom, but it's sooooooo hard."

"I know, sweetie. You will rock it. Be confident and believe! Your faith will be rewarded. Hey, I want to get these DNA samples in the mail today, so I'm going to run by the post office. Talk to you later? Love you!"

"Love you too, Liza!" We both brought our smoochy lips close to the front-facing camera and laughed at each other before I pushed the red button to end the call.

I left my house, and five minutes later I arrived at the post office. The roads were free from snow even though yards in my quiet neighborhood had remnants of the winter storm that passed through a few days earlier. The sun barely peeked out from behind fluffy white clouds and added just a touch of warmth to the 20°F winter air.

I deposited my destiny into the curbside mailboxes. Once I returned home, I called my oldest daughter, Capris, to see what she had on her plate for the weekend.

"Hey, Pretty."

"Hi, Mom!" Capris replied. People have always given me a hard time about the silent *s* on the end of her name. I blame it on all the French influence I had while studying the language in high school and college. It was either that or the drugs they gave me during childbirth. I am a huge fan of uncommon names, and for me, it would not have been the same if I would have spelled it Capri or Capree—so silent *s* it is.

"What are you doing?" I asked.

"I decided to coach a volleyball team."

"Oh really? What age group?"

"They're in eighth grade but will have to play in the 14s age bracket because some of them will be fourteen by next September," Capris said.

"You'll be competing against high schoolers."

"Yeah, but we'll play in Silver tournaments, so hopefully it won't be that bad."

Our family had been fully immersed in the local volleyball scene for the previous thirteen years. Capris's volleyball career started at the YMCA when she was ten years old. She went on to compete at the club, high school, and collegiate levels. This would be her first stint as head coach. Candace followed in her sister's footsteps as a player but stopped after high school.

Playing a sport changes the social aspect of college, and she wanted to focus on her studies instead of missing classes and always trying to play catch up. James and I loved being volleyball parents and spectators and I also enjoyed coaching at the YMCA and for club volleyball. We traveled the country for tournaments and met many lifelong friends along the way. Once we became empty nesters, my husband and I joked about finding someone else's kids to support so we could still get our volleyball fix.

"Let me know your schedule once you get it and your dad and I will come to some of your tournaments."

"I'll let you know. It's just a regional team, no traveling. What are you up to?" Capris asked.

"I just mailed off my DNA tests today."

"I didn't know you ordered any."

"I saw it on TV and just decided to do it. I'll get the results back in a few weeks. It should be interesting."

"Let me know how it turns out."

"For sure!"

"All right, I'm going to finish up my practice plan. Talk to you later?"

"Yep! Love you, sweetie!" I said.

"Looooove you," Capris replied.

In a few weeks, I would know my ethnicity and learn about diseases I might be prone to contracting. Whenever I went to the doctor, my standard response was always "unknown" when asked about medical conditions that ran in my family. Knowledge of inherited genetic factors could encourage me to make lifestyle changes, if needed, so seeing those reports was of utmost importance to me.

All that was left was to wait.

Capris, Lisa, Candace, James

CHAPTER 3

Ancestry Revealed

JANUARY 16, 2018, 10:50 A.M. "Your AncestryDNA results are in!" read the email subject line. I didn't hesitate to log in to my Ancestry account to review my DNA Story. I didn't know what to expect but I knew the curiosity about my ethnicity would soon be satisfied. Here's how Ancestry broke it down:

Korea/Northern China	50%
Benin/Togo	26%
Cameroon, Congo, Southern Bantu Peoples	9%
Ivory Coast/Ghana	7%
England, Wales, NW Europe	6%
Mali	2%

Next, I looked at my DNA matches. I had one hundred 4th cousins or closer. Ancestry rated each match and assigned them a confidence score ranging from extremely high to moderate. Any match that they categorized as extremely high meant the pair shared enough DNA to prove the individuals had a common recent ancestor. I had multiple matches in the extremely high confidence category:

CLOSE FAMILY – 1st COUSINS
Nicholas
Shared DNA: 1,809 cM across 72 segments

2nd COUSIN
Hbrow
Shared DNA: 335 cM across 23 segments

3rd COUSIN
Roy
Shared DNA: 142 cM across 9 segments

Nicholas and I shared the most segments and total centimorgans (cM), or small pieces of DNA. I took a deeper look and compared our ethnicity composition:

YOU		NICHOLAS
26%	Benin/Togo	29%
9%	Cameroon/Congo	27%
7%	Ivory Coast/Ghana	15%
6%	England/NW Europe	15%
2%	Mali	5%

We didn't match on the rest of the regions. I did the same comparison for the other six individuals in the extremely high confidence category and they all matched on the African regions. My primary focus had been centered around locating my birth mother. The potential for finding paternal relatives never hit my radar until that moment.

My phone rang while I reviewed the information.

"Sissy!" The familiar voice rang clear through the speaker. We'd been best friends since we were twelve years old. Our birthdays were five days apart, we were high school cheerleaders on the same squad, got our first jobs together, and had been there for each other during the best and worst of times. That's why we called each other Sissy whenever we talked to and texted one another.

"Hey, I got my Ancestry results back!"

"And?" she replied.

"I am half-Black and half-Korean, just like I was told."

"Yep, we knew that. Go on." She paused.

"It also tells me who my DNA matches are."

"Ok, Sissy, what's that?"

"It's people who Ancestry thinks you're related to. This first one—it says that we are first cousins."

"Ooooh really?"

"Yeah!"

"How can they tell?" she asked.

"We have shared DNA. There's over a hundred people who they identified I share DNA with, but this one is the closest in relation. There's one second cousin, one third cousin, and everyone else is fourth cousin or higher."

"Wow," she said.

"I know, isn't this crazy? They all match on the African region."

"So that's your dad's side."

"Yeah. But you know, this one right here—the one that says first cousin—the amount of shared DNA is so much more than all of the rest."

"Hmmm…" she said.

"You know, I don't think he's a cousin—he's a brother."

"You think so?"

"Yeah, I do, I really do."

"Why do you think that?"

"Because when I look at the shared DNA numbers, it's 1,809 cM, whatever that is, and 72 segments. I'm not sure what that means, but the next closest person, who is a second cousin, is 335 cM and 23 segments. That's a huge difference," I said.

"I see what you are saying. Where is he?"

"Not sure. It doesn't give me a location. It says the last time he logged in was on my dad's birthday, August 12, 2017. That was five months ago." I clicked on a couple more links on the website to get a better analysis of our estimated relationship.

"It tells you all that?"

"Yeah. I can send him a message through the Ancestry site, but since it's been so long since he logged in, he might not even see it."

"Yeah…" She released a small sigh.

"I guess if he has it set up so that he gets email notifications, then maybe he'll see it. Speaking of which, I need to check my settings to see if I get notifications." I clicked on my email settings under my account preferences and made sure I had email notifications turned on.

"I'm going to message everyone in the extremely high category."

"What are you going to say?" she asked.

"That I was adopted, and I am looking for my birth family."

"Let me know if they respond!"

"I will. Talk to you soon."

"All right, Sissy, love ya!"

"Love you too!" I hung up the phone.

It was a shot in the dark, but I composed my first message to Nicholas.

 Li Quaites
Jan 16, 2018

> Hi Nicholas! My name is Li Quaites and I recently used Ancestry to find out my DNA results. According to their findings, we are extremely likely to be 1st cousins! I was adopted when I was 2 yrs old, so I am looking for my birth family. All I know is that my dad was an African American service man who was in Seoul South Korea in 1966 or 1967. Does this sound like anyone in your family? Any information you can provide will be most helpful! Looking forward to hearing from you!

I sent a similar message to the other six matches in the extremely high confidence category. I prayed that someone would respond with pertinent information.

Internet research helped me to understand the DNA reports. I learned that cM (centimorgan) is the unit of measure used to determine the length of a DNA strand. Segments equate to the number of areas on the chromosome where the DNA between you and your match are identical. You can match in multiple locations on the same chromosome. That's why Ancestry shows the number of segments where DNA is identical to that of another individual.

The cell is the smallest structural and functional unit within the body of a human. It contains a nucleus which houses genetic material that is organized into chromosomes. The twenty-three pairs of genes that form each chromosome contain strands of deoxyribonucleic acid, most commonly known as DNA. These molecules carry genetic instructions used for growth, development, function, and reproduction of living organisms. The genes come in pairs, which we inherit from each parent. When one copy of the gene that we inherit from our mother differs from the copy of that same gene that we inherit from our father, at the same spot on the chromosome, that variant is referred to as an allele. These alleles determine the dominant and recessive traits that we inherit from our parents.

It is common to have some matching DNA with someone who is not a relative if they share the same ethnicity or come from the same region as you. That is why the confidence score is so important when determining kinship. Ancestry's confidence score considers the amount of shared DNA and whether most people would match at that allele. If the likelihood of a match at that location is rare, then it increases the confidence score.

Ancestry, which is available in four continents and thirty-six countries, boasts its database is ten million tests strong.

Although South Korea was one of the available countries, it presented no DNA relationship matches for me in that region. How disappointing, especially since I was searching for my birth mother. I had hoped I would have matched with a maternal relative.

I found Ancestry's migration information fascinating. It stated that from 1800 to 1825, Africans were kidnapped from their homeland and transported to America and the Caribbean islands. Most worked on sugar plantations. Slavery was abolished in Barbados between 1834 and 1838. From 1850 to 1900, Barbadians emigrated to Trinidad for better wages. According to Ancestry, the Panama Canal recruiting headquarters was set up in Barbados in 1903. Other Barbadians moved to the US and settled in Manhattan and Harlem in New York City.

Sleep that night was difficult to come by. I rested my head on the pillow, waiting for dormancy. Minutes passed like hours. Eventually I drifted off thinking about cells and chromosomes and DNA matches and Africa.

I HAD ONE MESSAGE in my Ancestry account when I logged in the next day.

Nicholas
Jan 16, 2018

Hi Li!
Thanks so much for reaching out. I may indeed have some info for you. My father is an African American man who spent time serving in Asia during the late 60's. He was never stationed in Seoul, but I think he mentioned having a relationship with someone from there. Do you know your birth mom's name?

Nick

I covered my gaping mouth with both of my hands. Tears welled up in my eyes. I read, reread, and read his message again. My heart confirmed to my brain the idea I had voiced yesterday—somehow, I *knew* Nicholas was my brother. I took a few minutes to get myself together before typing a reply.

Li Quaites
Jan 17, 2018

OMG Nick thank you so much for replying! I must admit I became a bit emotional when reading your message, because I feel that it is one step closer to finding my birth family. I do not know the name of either parent. All I know is that my mother is Korean and may have lived in or near Seoul, since that is where I was dropped off at an orphanage in July of 1969. My US Naturalization documents lists my birth date as August 10, 1967. Someone who knew me well dropped me off because my first medical exam had specific information such as me walking at 10 months of age and being breastfed for the first year. But all of the adoption paperwork said that my mother and father are unknown. What is your father's name and what is the name of the Asian woman he had a relationship with? Was she Korean? Any other information you can provide is most helpful. When submitting my DNA to Ancestry, I used the name that was on my adoption paperwork (Augustine Lee) but I am not certain that is my birth name. Feel free to call or email me if you want to talk further, or you can continue to use ancestry messaging, either way it works for me. Thanks again for the info. I have hope!!

Within minutes, I received a text.

Wed, Jan 17, 2:11 PM

Hi Li, this is Nick. Just saw your last message. I think a phone call would probably serve you best at this point. What's your availability tomorrow morning? Like 8-9am central?

> Hi Nick! I am available and look forward to speaking with you!!

> Great! I'll call around 8:30a

I was anxious to tell James about the digital conversation I had with Nick.

"Wow, he must have some information for you if he's recommending a call!" said James.

"Right! He knows something for sure," I said.

My mind raced thinking about a conversation that would happen in less than twelve hours. I struggled through another sleepless night, tossing and turning, while pondering the ways my life could change. But how could I fathom the possibilities when I had no clue what was going to be discussed? One thing was certain—God was in control. I prayed for Him to step in and take over. I had no way of knowing what was in store, but God had always taken care of me. Even when I didn't realize I needed to be taken care of. He had always shown me mercy and grace, so I said a prayer of gratitude, thanking Him for what He had already done in my life and for what He was going to do in the future.

CHAPTER 4

The Call

THE NEXT MORNING, I rose before the sun. Too excited to sleep and too nervous to focus my attention on any one thing, I looked at the clock every few minutes to make sure I didn't miss The Call.

"Hello?" I paused before repeating the greeting. "Hello?"

"Hello hello," replied Nick with a deep voice.

"Hello, Nick, how are you?" I said.

"Good. How are you doing?" said Nick.

"I'm doing good. Thank you for calling. I have my husband James here with me too."

"How are you doing, Nick?" said James.

"Good, good, nice to meet you."

"Nice to meet you too," James and I responded simultaneously.

"My wife is here too. Anna-Marie."

"Hi, Anna-Marie, how are you?" I said as James said hello. The mobile phone technology caused her faint greeting to fade in and out.

"I'm so excited to talk to you guys." A nervous laugh became audible as I tried to keep my composure. I repositioned myself on my kitchen bar stool.

"I'm glad you hit me up. I'll jump right in with what I know," Nick said. "I think that we are half siblings."

I mentally processed what I heard and allowed my inner calm to have an external release with a soft "Ok."

"I think you are my father's firstborn child. Based on what you said when you sent me your first message a couple of days ago, I reached out to him and asked him to corroborate any of it. He said he was in a relationship with a Korean woman named Chung Suk-ah."

I finally learned my mother's name! This simple thing was monumental for me. I wrote it down in my notebook, but her name was instantly engraved on my heart.

"And he said she is from the village of Nul No Ri. He knew that you were born sometime in the summer of '67—in July or August."

"Oh my gosh, ok, so…." I was unable to mask the astonishment in my voice, because even though we'd been speaking for three minutes and twenty-one seconds at that point, it had suddenly just become real. That statement validated in my mind that Nick was telling the truth and that I was in fact his father's firstborn child.

"He said he has two pictures of you and your mom."

"OH MY GOSH!" The words slipped from my mouth as my eyes welled up with tears. My raw emotion surfaced when I thought about the possibility of seeing the pictures that my newfound brother had mentioned. My husband's consoling rub on my back didn't stop the flow of tears.

"Yep, and—" Nick tried to continue speaking but paused to allow me a few seconds to soak in the information he gave me. He did his best to speak around my sobs. "He mentioned never seeing you in person."

Bigger sobs escaped, despite my best effort to stifle them. My dog, Boomer, sensed I was having an emotional episode. Whining accompanied his concerned puppy dog eyes as he hovered near the base of my chair.

"Ok." My shaky voice managed to enunciate an emotional sigh. James handed me some tissues and I wiped my tear-drenched cheeks before Nick continued.

"I also did a little more digging on Ancestry, and if you look at the numbers behind our genetics, we have 1800 units in common. Per the website, that is indicative of you being either my grandparent, my aunt, or my half sibling. We're in the half-sibling range in terms of the rating, and Ancestry's confidence level is extremely high, so the likelihood that we're half siblings is 100 percent."

Sobs interrupted my silent absorption of the information. My thoughts were all over the board, and I had difficulty collecting them into any type of coherent phrase. Sensing this, James piped up and asked, "Nick, what made you decide to take the DNA test?"

"I kind of did it for my dad's side. He's from Barbados and grew up in the Caribbean. Our dad always talked about origins in Ireland because there were so many Irish sugarcane plantations on his island. I was just trying to see how far back that was."

I let out a small joyful gasp. Nick said "our dad." I also delighted in the fact that I was Caribbean and Korean. I never imagined my family tree could have tropical roots.

I didn't appreciate my mixed ethnicity as a child. No one I knew looked like me, and kids were mean. I was bullied in early elementary school because my classmates were either White or Black. They made it clear to me that I was neither.

I never experienced racism from any of my immediate or extended family members. They accepted me as their own and when I looked in the mirror, a little Black girl stared back at me. That's why my second-grade brain could not comprehend why my peers called me "China Girl" and used their fingers to stretch the corners of their eyes out and upward.

Nick continued, "I also wanted to do it with my wife because she's half-Asian and half-White. Her mom's from the

Philippines, and they are very mixed up as a people too. Never looked into it more after we got our results."

Nick paused for a moment, allowing James and I time to mentally process. We exchanged glances and I knew we were on the same thought path. *Timing is everything!* If Nick had not done his DNA test five months earlier, we may have never found out about each other.

"Was that your reason, Li, for doing Ancestry? To find a lot of that out?" Nick asked.

I wanted to know my ethnicity and was curious about inherited traits that could trigger health-related issues. And if my birth parents were still alive, they weren't getting any younger and neither was I. I'd love to meet them, if that was something that they wanted to do. If not, that was cool too, because if I were some sort of secret, I wasn't trying to disrupt anybody's life, fifty years later.

I didn't know if my biological dad knew I existed. Perhaps he never knew my mom was pregnant, or maybe my biological mom didn't know who my father was. Finding out that my dad knew about me, and that he had a relationship with my mom, and it wasn't just a one-night stand or the result of a nonconsensual incident, was comforting to me.

Korean culture in the late 1960s didn't accept mixed-race children. I would not have been able to have the family name or get a job, no Korean man would have found me worthy of marriage, and I would have lived on the bottom rung of the nation's social ladder.

"I don't know if my mother is still alive. I don't know if our dad knows...." My voice tapered as I tried to control the emotions welling up inside of me.

"I want to thank my mom for her sacrifice and let her know I turned out ok." Tears streamed freely down my cheeks. My husband rubbed my back, consoling me as I whimpered.

"It's good that we got to contact each other. While he didn't raise me, there's like seven or eight of us total," Nick said.

"Oh my!" It never occurred to me that I would have so many siblings. The flow of tears slowed down.

"That was going to be my next question," James said.

Before Nick continued, Anna-Marie said, "For the longest time, my husband thought he was one of six, until December 2016 when his German half sibling came to the States. She was over to Dad's house and was like, 'Oh, it's so good to finally meet the oldest of us.' She was referring to your Japanese brother. But that is when your dad told them about you," Anna-Marie said.

"We found out that you were a person twelve months ago," Nick said.

"OH MY GOSH!" My laughter came from deep within. "OH MY GOSH!"

"It was crazy! I meant to ask you: Was your adoptive father in the army?" Nick asked.

"No, he was air force," I said.

"Our dad was stationed in Okinawa while he was in the army."

I would later discover that my adoptive dad and my biological father were both stationed at separate military bases in Okinawa in 1970. It blew my mind to learn my birth father and I were only separated by a few miles when he was twenty-one years old.

"His son, Anthony, was born in Okinawa, and that is who I thought was my oldest sibling. Dad married that brother's mom, but I don't know the stories behind all his relationship get-togethers and breakups. Then Dad went to Germany and, between two different women, had three more kids. After that is when he returned to the United States. He retired from the army after serving ten years, then married my mom and had me and our younger sister. She and I both grew up with my mother. Dad moved five doors down from us after he and my mom divorced."

I loved the way Nick made reference to *our* younger sister.

"That is something," James said.

"Yep," responded Nick. "Our dad just turned seventy-one. His birthday is December 1, so he was born in 1945 or 46, whatever it is." Anna-Marie's giggling in the background suggested mental math was not my brother's strong suit. Mine either, for that matter.

Nick continued on, "Dad moved to Peoria after retiring from the US military. Now he's a psychotherapist helping to rehabilitate kids that didn't attach to their parents properly. But he's a funny guy. If you get credit for being the life of the party or making friends easily, it's probably from his side. And he's a showman by nature. His grandfather was a traveling entertainer of some sort," Nick said.

"Really?" James asked.

"Yeah, I guess it's like a gene, an entertainer gene."

Fascinating bit of family history.

"What else do you want to know? We just had our fourth child, a week and a half ago," said Nick.

"Wow, congratulations! Do you have girls or boys?" I said.

"We have two girls and two boys. Our oldest is Alexandria and she'll be four in March," Nick said.

Four-year-olds are my favorite. They are past the terrible twos and threes stage, and the thoughts their budding brains produce amuse me.

"Our oldest son, Gideon, will be three in June. And then Olivia Joy is one-and-a-half," Nick said.

I did the math. My brother had four children, no multiple births, and the oldest was three years old. How awesome!

"I can tell you about your other siblings if you want to know."

"Yeah, absolutely." I sat up straighter in my chair, with my mechanical pencil in hand, ready to write as if I were taking notes for an exam.

"I'm not that close with the three of them that remain in Illinois. Anthony, Nadine, and Rob all live near our dad in

Peoria," Nick said. I wrote all of that down in my notebook to ensure I had it to look back on later.

"Same dad, but different mom?" I interrupted Nick before he finished his thought.

"Our dad, but Nadine and Rob have the same mom." Nick paused so Anna-Marie could speak.

"When your dad was in Europe, he had a relationship with an American woman, and he had a son and daughter by her. During that time, he had a relationship with a German woman, which resulted in your sister Diana being born in between Nadine and Rob. She still lives in Germany. Then he followed the American woman to Illinois, but her family didn't like Black guys, so it was tough for him to keep that relationship," Anna-Marie said.

"Was she White?" I asked.

"She's White, yes," Anna-Marie continued. "They ended up separating, and eventually he got with Nick's mom. Nick never had a relationship with those two siblings. He knew Anthony because he lived with your dad for a while." That was a lot of information to absorb.

"Is Rob Dad's son too?" I asked. Even with my notes, it was getting difficult to keep track of how everyone was connected. Cerebral overload ensued as I tried to recall names, ages, events, and relationships.

"Yep. I'm not sure about everyone's ages, but Devin is the youngest and she just turned twenty-five in November. I'm thirty-two. Rob's probably around thirty-five. Going off of when Diana was here, she said she was thirty-six. Nadine must be almost forty. Anthony isn't too much younger than you.

"Not sure what they do professionally. In my adult life, I've only seen Rob one time. He was bartending at a place where I was celebrating with friends," Nick said.

"Nadine was a professional dancer for a while," Anna-Marie said. Our great-grandfather's entertainer genes were alive and well.

"But she recently had a couple of kids. Um…what else? Anthony has two kids too, a daughter and son," Nick said.

Anna-Marie continued, "After your dad split from his mom, she sent Anthony to Germany. They annulled so she could remarry in Japan without any shame."

"Sure, ok. Shoot, how many times was Dad married?" Between us seven kids, I counted five different mothers.

"Um…that's a good question! He was married to Anthony's mom. He was married to Nadine's mom, or was that Diana's mom?" Anna-Marie helped Nick think through the facts.

"He was married to one of the German relationships for sure. He married my mom and they got divorced when I was two. And then he married his current wife, but they don't have any children together."

"Okay, so that is four?"

"Four, I guess, yep." Nick confirmed my count was correct.

"And you said he's originally from Barbados?" I asked.

"Yeah, he was born and raised in Barbados, but spent his teenage years in New York. We went there with him a couple of years ago to meet a lot of his cousins. His siblings and some other cousins have either moved from Barbados or passed away. His mom died in 2010. She moved to New York when Dad was a young boy and worked as a nurse. She would send money and clothes back to Barbados to support the family there. Dad lived with his grandmother until he was sixteen, and that is when his mom came back and moved him and his siblings, along with the grandmother that Dad had been living with, to New York. After arriving in the United States, he finished high school, and then as soon as he got done, he went into the army," Nick said.

"This is so crazy! You may not know, but did he give any more details about his relationship with my mom?"

"He did not."

"Do you think he would either send you or send me the

pictures he has of me and my mom? I'd like to see pictures of the whole family. And of course, if Dad wants, I would also like to be in contact with him." A nervous chuckle followed my words.

My mother's face had eluded my dreams for fifty years. My curiosity was piqued. Did I look like my siblings? Would there be any trace of family resemblance in the features or mannerisms of these people with whom I shared DNA?

"Yeah, I'll ask him. I'm sure he won't have an issue with the pictures or any of that, I'll just hit him up and ask what he wants to do," Nick said.

"Ok, that sounds good. THIS IS INCREDIBLE. I'll tell you guys that this right here is prayers answered. I cannot begin to tell you how good God has been to me!"

I didn't live in that orphanage for very long before being adopted. My parents told me they sifted through pictures of eligible candidates. Children who had no permanent home or forever family. They had chosen a little girl, but she had a sibling and the orphanage wanted to keep them together. The pair ended up getting adopted by another family. So my parents chose another little girl who was around six years old—roughly the same age as their youngest son, Miles. But when it came time for them to meet her, she had already made up her mind that she did not want to be adopted. She knew who her mother was, and she was hoping her mother would come back to the orphanage to get her. Since my parents were there in Seoul, the chaplain asked the agency if there were any other eligible girls that were ready for adoption and that is when the orphanage sent me to meet them.

My adoptive parents, Clayton and Mildred, are originally from Kentucky. They are super sweet people, but they didn't choose me. I was not their first choice; I was not their second choice. It was God that decided I was going to become a part of their family.

"I've been praying for years to meet my biological family if it is God's will. I'm happy and humbled that He decided to let it be so." Emotion surged within me, like an ocean wave defying gravity as it reaches up toward heaven, preparing to crash onto the sandy shore upon its descent.

Between whimpers I said, "I look forward to meeting you guys. I look forward to meeting my other siblings, meeting Dad, and seeing if I can contact Mom. I don't even know if she's still alive." I continued on through sniffles, "I just look forward to establishing those relationships. I look forward to you guys meeting my family and the people God surrounded me with, because He surrounded me with awesome people. And I'm so thankful."

My emotions took control and found release from my internal barricades that failed to keep them contained. Those restraints were no match for that ocean wave, which hit shore on tear-stained cheeks.

I never ever thought I would find my birth father. Never dreamed he would be from Barbados; I thought he was American. I'd often thought about him being in the US, but I didn't realize how DNA testing increased the odds of finding relatives. Now it seemed finding my mom's side was going to be a challenge. But I had hope in knowing that she and Dad had a relationship. He could tell me things about her, and I was extremely interested in seeing those pictures.

"How strong is your connection to Korean culture? Do you know people who can help you translate any of those documents that you have? We have some good friends that could help with that," said Nick.

"The documents are already translated because I've got the Korean copy and then I've got the copy that's in English. But now that I have the village name where my mom once lived, that will help a lot too," I said.

Nick continued, "Diana will be super excited to talk to you. I'll connect you guys through social media. It's cool that you reached out, and you're always welcome to come and see us here. We live fifteen minutes from O'Hare Airport. Whenever you want to make time, we'll be here, changing diapers." Laughter erupted from all of us.

"What do you guys do for a living?" I asked.

"I just retired two years ago. I was playing football and had to stop when I got hurt. Now I'm at home full-time with the babies. And Anna-Marie is halfway through massage therapy school. She'll be done with that in the summertime. But I'm just making dinner and doing dishes and stuff." Nick's laughter at the end of his statement gave us a sneak peek at his good-natured personality.

"How old are your kids?" Anna-Marie asked.

I responded that our oldest daughter, Capris, turned twenty-three in November. She attended Drake University in Des Moines, Iowa, on an athletic scholarship and got hired to work for Principal Financial Group after graduation. She was part of their Leadership Development Program, where they worked six-month rotations in different parts of the company within a three-year time period. She was on her second rotation and brushing up on her Spanish to improve her chances of securing an international position.

Candace had just turned twenty and was a sophomore at KU in Lawrence, Kansas, pursuing an undergraduate pre-pharmacy track. The university attracted her because of its six-year PharmD program and the quaint college town which surrounded the campus. If the pharmacy school approved her application, she would start in the fall.

James's thirty-six year old son, Chris, lived in Georgia with his wife and their two kids. My oldest adoptive brother, Clayton, a US navy retiree, also lived in Georgia with his wife.

Our other brother, Miles, was five years older than me, but he passed away in 2007 of an enlarged heart. My dad, Clayton, and mom, Mildred, lived in Omaha. They were going to celebrate a major milestone in June of that year. Sixty-three years of marital bliss. In May, James and I, Capris, Candace,

Clayton, and his wife planned to celebrate with them in Honolulu, Hawaii.

"How awesome! That's a long time!" said Nick.

"Yes. It. Is!"

My emphasis on each word made us all laugh. In the military culture, parents were held accountable for the actions of their children. That ethos fostered his strict disciplinarian parenting style and controlling demeanor. Growing up in his household wasn't easy. I didn't understand it then, but when I became an adult I realized he raised my brothers and me the best way he knew how, and we all survived and grew up to be responsible adults.

When I moved out of his home, our relationship improved. I no longer had to abide by his rules, and I escaped his criticism and scrutiny—most of the time. Our houses were within five minutes driving distance and having active grandparents available to my children was a tremendous blessing.

In the '60s, my parents had two sons, and they longed for a daughter. My mom had several miscarriages, which prompted the decision to adopt when the opportunity was presented to them by the base chaplain.

Telling them that I'd located my biological father would be interesting. Since that was such an unexpected discovery, I didn't have time to think about how that revelation would affect them. I never considered if it would hurt their feelings or if they would think my actions betrayed their forever love for me. I didn't entertain the possibility they would become angry or jealous. Those thoughts never crossed my mind, and even if they had, they wouldn't have been a deterrent nor hinderance toward my quest to find my birth mother. My parents had given me the name of the adoption agency and my documentation, so in my mind, that served as approval for me to research my past.

"Cool, do you guys have any more questions for me?" asked Nick.

"Are there family reunions on our dad's side?" I asked.

"Not on our dad's side, because everyone is so spread out, but we have a gigantic family reunion on my mom's side every summer."

Anna-Marie mentioned that her father-in-law goes to it. Nick confirmed. "Yeah, our dad will be there with his wife."

I was a little surprised but glad that our dad had maintained a good relationship with Nick's mother and her family.

"You guys are welcome to come to that. It's a whoever-has-found-themselves-to-be-called-family type of gathering. We'll have a big smoker going for a couple of days, fish fries, and you know, all that stuff," Nick said.

"Is that there in Chicago?" James asked.

"Every other year it's in Peoria. This year it's August 2–5. It's a Thursday through Sunday," Nick said.

I wrote those dates in my notes. "And your siblings go to that?"

"Definitely me and my sister—err, our sister, Devin. Probably not Nadine and Rob," said Nick.

"Anthony comes sometimes," Anna-Marie said.

"Yeah, Anthony might be there. Most of the time he's there at least one day. Oh yeah, my dad will be there. Err, our dad. Sorry I keep saying that," Nick corrected himself.

"That's ok! It's something to get used to!" I said.

"Yeah, it's a good time and it's casual. Just chilling and eating and hanging out," Nick continued. "I actually have another brother on my mom's side. He's forty-two. The result of a high school relationship my mom had with a different guy. The three of us are the closest of all of my siblings since we grew up together with my mom."

"Might have to plan a trip." The world suddenly became so small. A seven-hour drive or an hour-and-a-half flight would put me on the doorstep of a biological relative.

"I'm glad you guys reached out, it's cool," said Nick.

"We look forward to meeting you and getting to know you

better. We don't want to bum-rush you with our excitement," James said. His animated arms moved as he spoke. I agreed with his sentiment.

Nick laughed. "Yeah, no problem. And don't be concerned, you won't bother us with questions. We're here if you need clarification or you want to know something a little deeper."

"Thank you. I am eternally grateful for you and I look forward to meeting the family. We'll be in touch again soon," I said. "Bye."

I pressed the red phone icon to end the most astonishing call of my life.

My Family Tree

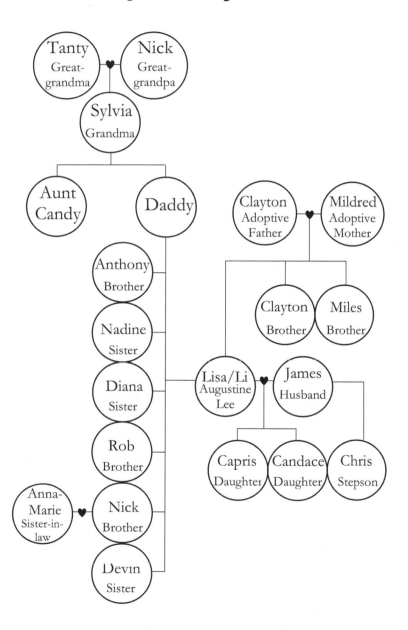

CHAPTER 5

International Relations

OUR SISTER DIANA IS three years younger than our sister Nadine. Her German mother met our dad after he got out of the army, but before he left Germany. I followed Nick's suggestion and reached out to her.

JAN 18, 10:53 AM

Hi Diana! I had an incredible conversation with Nick and Anna-Marie this morning and we believe I am your long lost older Korean sister! Please message me back so we can get to know each other and put the puzzle pieces together. Looking forward to hearing from you!

Hi

Where are you?

Which one is you???

So excited !!!

JAN 18, 1:02 PM

I live in the US in Omaha, Nebraska. I haven't had any contact with Dad yet but I would love to if he is willing. Nick is going to reach out to him and get back with me.

Sure he will

That's great you are in the US

I am in Germany

How old are you?

50

Do you have a pic of yourself?

I am 37

So happy too hear from you.

We heard about you last year. I was at dad's house for Christmas and I asked him if Tony is the oldest one. Then he told us about you.

> He was very
> emotional. Said he
> didn't know if you
> survived. So I was
> praying since then
> you are alive

Christians use prayer to talk to God. Intercessory prayer, when someone prays on behalf of others, changes lives, breaks down barriers, and restores strength. My sister's expression of agape love created an eternal bond between sisters who had yet to meet.

I sent Diana a selfie I took on my 50th birthday. My long dark hair, flat ironed straight and parted on the side, swept over the rims of my glasses. My skin was still sun-kissed from the Caribbean cruise I had returned from just a week prior. Many of my friends celebrated the half-century milestone birthday that year, and a couple of girlfriends and I elected to revel all year long.

> You wear his face!
>
> Oh my God!
>
> You are so pretty 😍 😊
> 😊
>
> Did you see a pic of
> him?

Diana sent me a picture of Daddy and our baby sister, Devin. They were standing cheek to cheek, smiling for the camera. I spent my entire life wondering what my parents looked like. I never thought the day would come when I'd find out. Daddy's milk chocolate skin was virtually wrinkle-free. Devin was a few shades lighter than Daddy, and a makeup-free beauty. We had the same eyelashes.

I am so emotional right now. Thank you so much for sending me this pic!! God is so good and he answers prayers!

This is Tony the 2nd

Me too

Crying like a baby😂

Send me your pic

Please 🥺

Do you have a pic of Nadine or Robert?

This is dini

The pictures were coming one right after the other, which didn't give me much time for in-depth analysis. The Blasian mix that Anthony and I shared gave our appearance a bit of natural likeness. Nadine's big smile revealed a tooth gap that mirrored one that both of my daughters had fixed with braces while they were teenagers.

Diana sent me two pictures of herself. The first one was of her standing in between two of her friends at an outdoor venue she vetted for her July 2019 nuptials. She warded off the briskness of winter with her knee-high boots, scarf, and coat. The second picture had been taken while she was at work. Her pink, white, and beige business attire complemented her fair skin. Her dark curls reminded me of mine whenever I chose to wear my hair natural instead of straightening it.

The next picture she sent was of Rob, who looked strikingly like Nadine. They shared a mom and the front tooth gap. I'd always blamed the gap my daughters had on my husband, but that likely came from my side of the family.

Wow I wish we could all get together for a group picture

Yes. I was so glad to meet Devin and Nadine and now you. That is awesome!

I told dad last year I am so happy about him having so many kids even he wasn't there! Look at you! Isn't that crazy?

I have pics of our grand ma. I must find them first. From Barbados. So excited!

I would love to see pics of grandma when you find them. Chat with you later! Hugs 🤗

Sure. Let's talk later. Happy you never gave up!

Less than six hours earlier, my entire life changed with the knowledge that I located my birth father and paternal siblings. Diana messaged me again about an hour later.

I talked to him. He is very happy to hear from you 😂😂😂😂😂 😂😂

Diana sent a picture of our great-grandma Tanty and grandma Sylvia. They were beautiful in their church attire. I couldn't stop looking at the generations in that photo. They were the ancestors who prayed for me. I hope they know God heard them.

PROCESSING ALL THAT I learned that day became a mental challenge. I messaged Devin and verified that she and Nick shared the same mom and our dad.

> Hahaha yes! We do. Actually Nick and I are very close so he told me about you when you first emailed him! Last year I got to meet Diana and Rob for the first time and I've wanted to meet all of my siblings so this is really exciting!

> Well we will meet soon and I will call you this weekend! Hugs 👻

> 😊😊😊 Yes! I'll actually be at Nick's this weekend. Maybe we can FaceTime if that works for you!

> Absolutely!! When will you be there?

I will be there tomorrow around 8 and I'll be there until Sunday. Let me know when you're free!

Ok I will text you. Safe travels and we'll "see" each other soon 😊

Late that night, exhaustion settled in. Long, hot, thirty-minute showers were my guilty pleasure. I stood underneath the square showerhead and closed my eyes. Serenity eased into my muscles as the water droplets drenched my skin. I did some of my best thinking and reflecting in my shower sanctuary.

James was asleep by the time I finished in the bathroom. I knelt beside my bed to petition God and offer gratitude for the day's disclosure.

Dear Heavenly Father, I come to you with a bowed head and humbled heart, and I thank you for the revelation that came to light today. Lord, thank you for allowing me to find my biological father and siblings. Dear Heavenly Father, what seems impossible for man is possible with you. So many things were working against me, but all I needed was you working for me. Dear Lord, you did not handpick me out of that orphanage for nothing. I still don't have a grasp on my own destiny, but Lord, I place it in your hands. Thank you for the miracles that you have manifested in my life. Thank you for the precious gifts that you have given to lowly me. Your word tells us that what God has for you is for you. I'm so thankful, Lord. I can't even begin to express it. But God, you see my heart. You know. I am in awe of your marvelous works. I am in awe of your goodness. Thank you, Lord, for having mercy upon me when I was in that orphanage. Thank you, Lord, for taking care of me. Thank you, Lord, for your grace. Thank you for bestowing blessings upon me that I didn't even know to ask for—your favor, Lord. While I have asked to find my mother, I've never asked to find my father, but you saw fit to make it happen. You are such a good God. I so humbly thank you, yet I know I can't thank you enough. I love you, Lord, and for these blessings and others, I do pray and ask it all in the sweet name of Jesus, AMEN.

I rose from my knees and crawled into bed. I had no issues sleeping that night, as my mind and body were drained.

I WOKE UP TO several messages from Diana, the last being an audio one.

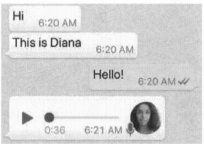

Diana: "It's so crazy…I'm the emotional one. I'm crying since yesterday. I'm so glad you're here. Let me know what he thinks about you. If you call Dad, he always has problem with his fingers and with the display. But he is happy to hear from you. He had all these questions I couldn't answer. And yeah, he's still working. I don't know what time it is at your place. In Germany it's 1:21 p.m."

Her German-accented English was superb. I responded back to her with my own audio message in English since my German vocabulary was limited to phrases—guten Tag and auf Wiedersehen.

Li: "Oh my gosh, Diana, it is so good to hear your voice. We sound similar. And we have the same hair. I'm going to send you a picture of me when I have curly hair. If Dad is working, that's ok, I can contact him later. It's 6:20 in the morning here in Omaha, and I think Dad and I are in the same time zone. This is CRAZY. Yesterday was a very emotional day for me as well. I am loving this, and I can't wait to get to know everybody. We will talk soon."

Our messaging continued with a mix of typed words and audio messages.

> Thanks for not giving up.
> Grandma would love to
> hear about you! She died 8
> years ago. But it still feels
> like she is around 😊
>
> 6:28 AM

Diana sent me a picture of her with her daughter. Their resemblance was strong, with the same honey-colored skin tone, dark facial features, and black curly hair.

Diana: "I grew up in Germany with my mother's children. I have an older sister, but she has a huge distance to us, and a younger brother. And all my siblings in the US—I got to meet Nicky when I was nine, and all the other ones I never met before last year. And with Facebook, I texted everybody, 'come on, let's have a dinner or lunch together,' because not everybody from our family wants to talk to Dad because he wasn't there for everybody—actually for nobody, but he's nice. He's a cute guy. Last Christmas, we all sat together for dinner, and it was great. I hope we can do it this year in July."

Li: "Wow, that is incredible. I had no idea that Dad wasn't involved in any of our siblings' lives. I'm glad we are all connected now, and I look forward to being able to spend time with everyone. I want to be included in everything, so please let me know whenever there are family gatherings or whatever is going on, that would be great. I grew up with two brothers, and I was the baby. And now to learn that I'm the oldest of seven…IT'S CRAZY!"

Diana: "I think it's great. Well, he was involved— he did call and send birthday cards, and he was aware of my grades, but he didn't have kids in his household. He pushed Nicky to the Chicago Bears, he pushed Devin for college. But you know, our dad is a Caribbean dad and they probably think different. He's not like a TV dad, or my stepdad here in Germany, who participates in a child's life. He wants to be part of his children's lives, he just didn't raise any of us after he split from our moms. He's seventy-one now and he's a very old-fashioned Caribbean man. But he's lots of fun. He loves to laugh, eat, drink, and dance. He has lots of sense of humor. He's very active, he can't sit still. It's crazy, being around him. It's exhausting, to me. Have you told your daughters?"

> I haven't mentioned any of this to them yet. They have such busy schedules and we all live in different cities. I am going to have a call with them tonight. I'll also tell my adoptive parents and Brother this weekend.
>
> 7:25 AM ✓✓

> And tell your parents thanks from all of us for treading you great 😊
>
> 7:27 AM

> Will do! They provided me with a very loving and stable home and I am eternally grateful to them for that!   7:28 AM ✓✓
>
> Me too 😄   7:29 AM

Around the same time, Rob responded via Messenger.

> JAN 19, 7:10 AM
>
> Hello Lisa. It was nice to hear from Diana that you'd gotten into contact. 😊 I look forward to getting to know you.
>
> JAN 19, 8:58 AM
>
> I would love that! It has been an extremely emotional 24 hours that's for sure! Let's try to chat this weekend.
>
> I don't have weekends off very often so feel free to message me and I will answer as soon as I can. I'm off to bed as I work later tonight. Ttys. 😊

Later that afternoon, I messaged Diana again. She was quick to respond, with the seven-hour time difference putting her at off-work hours. Her fountain of knowledge about the family was endless and I appreciated the outpouring and her eagerness to share.

Diana: "Have you seen Nick's babies? They're sooo cute. And they're Asian mix as well. And Anthony's—since he's half Japanese, his daughter and son have bright skin."

Diana sent me a picture of Anthony's children. Their light complexion prompted me to ask if their mother was White.

Diana: "I've never met her, but yes, she's White. Dini and Robert's mom is White too. My mom is White. Nicki and Devin's mom—she's Black. When will you Facetime Dad? Is your heart bumpin'?"

I responded via audio message that Dad wanted to FaceTime a few hours later. I told her that I was excited, but unusually calm.

I love your voice   2:18 PM

You actually sound like dini   2:18 PM

Thank you! And really?? Even though you have an accent, there are times when I think you and I sound similar   2:19 PM

What do you do for living?   2:19 PM

I am Technology Director for 2 commercial real estate companies. I fix people's computer and mobile phone problems all day 😊   2:21 PM

Are you a happy person? On the pics you seem active and a fun person   2:21 PM

Li: "Yes, I am a happy person. I love to have a good time. I found it funny when you said that Dad's always on the go and it wears you out. I must get it from him. It's common for me to have a million things on my plate. I like to laugh. I'm easygoing. I just can't wait for you to get to know me and my personality, and for me to know you as well."

Diana: "Don't play with me! Are you serious? C'mon! You know what? Um, oh my god! Listen, a couple weeks ago, on Christmas, my sweet boyfriend asked me to marry him after seven long years. He lives and works in Switzerland, and I live in Germany, and since seven years we have that relationship long distance. And he wants to come back home. His family is thirty minutes by car from here. He's trying to get a job here. Nadine asked me just a couple of hours ago what dresses I like and if I already have a date. I would prefer to get married next year in 2019 so I have more time to save money. Because I like to have a nice party and good food and I want some nice alcohol and good party, party, party. I would LOVE for you guys to come over. Oh my god, I need a good hotel!"

Li: "Oh my gosh, Diana, that is so exciting, congratulations! I am soooo happy for you. I'm gonna be there. You tell me when and where. It's interesting, because James and I celebrated our twenty-fifth wedding anniversary last April, and I wanted to plan a trip to Europe. James has never been out of the country, but I have. I tried hard to plan that trip, but it didn't work, and we ended up going somewhere else. So I told him, 2019, I want to go to Europe, and he said ok. And we haven't planned the trip or anything, but I told him yesterday, after messaging you, I figured out why I couldn't make that trip work last year. Because God had other things planned. He knew that we were going to be going to Germany to spend time with my sister. I didn't know that back then, but He knew. So yes, it is in the plan, you just need to let me know when and where and we will be on that jet."

Diana: "And you're a Believer too? I always thought I'm the only one in this whole family from my mom's side and dad's side, except Grandma. She's a Believer too. I'm two hours by train from Paris, four hours from Switzerland. I am six hours from Italy. Four or five hours from Belgium. Hamburg is five hours. Frankfurt is one hour. You can plan your trip from here."

Li: "We will definitely do that. If there's anything you want me to do for your wedding, let me know. I love party planning. I'm the event planner for the family."

Diana: "Oh, I can tell you what you can do for me. I need physical touch. You can give me a hug to calm me down. I hate organizing parties. I love partying and parties, but just the thought of organizing this wedding….and my fiancé, he has a pretty high standard. He wants everything really cool and extravagant. I just want good food. I want a good mood and nice people around me. I like good relationships and have a good time and he wants all this extra stuff. I just need a dress, you know. Everything is on me now and I hate organizing. I don't want to say hate, I just don't like it and I'm stressed out. So first we planned the wedding for September of this year, but I told him, hey, I can't do it. I just can't. I'm going to show you a few things, like the location. I wanted to get the wedding in a real castle, but I couldn't find one close to this area, so I don't have a location, I don't have a date. Now I'm going to start with a dress next week. I'm going through a designer. She does it…I don't know if you say it in English like that…from scratch? That's where I start. But yes, I need hugs. Hugs!"

What followed next were twenty-five pictures of venues that Diana had visited and Pinterest links to wedding gown examples and decoration ideas. Many of the links were in German, reminding me of our language difference, which was easy to overlook since Diana's English was so good. I loved weddings, and if I had another career choice, event planning would be in the top five options. I liked the organization and coordination required to pull off a successful event.

As Diana and I ended our conversation for the day, I noticed that Nadine responded to my initial message. Getting to know my new siblings was a fun experience. They all welcomed me and were open to establishing relationships.

I couldn't be more grateful. I've heard stories of newly discovered family members being shunned or not welcomed. Rejection is always a risk, but in this case, it was not my reality with my paternal relatives.

I knew, however, that family honor was paramount for Koreans, and babies born out of wedlock brought shame upon the entire family. I didn't know if I would ever connect with a maternal relative or if I would ever be accepted by them. But I was willing to continue my quest and take the risk.

CHAPTER 6

Daddy & Umma

NICK TEXTED ME A contact labeled 'Daddy.' I now had his phone number, and I was ready for our first conversation. I didn't know what to think or how to feel. Anticipation grew over seeing my birth father's face, studying his mannerisms, and hearing his voice.

I took a deep breath. A slow, steady exhalation helped calm my mind and body. I stared at Daddy's phone number on my iPad screen. What the heck was I supposed to say when he answered the video call? How should I introduce myself? Was it going to be awkward? Was I ready for this?

Daddy answered the call. His broad toothy smile stretched across his face. He laughed with delight at seeing me on his screen. I reciprocated with my own broad toothy smile.

"Ahhh, sweetheart!" The words took a minute to release from his lips, but when they fell upon my ears, decades of wondering vanished.

"Hi, Daddy!" The little girl in me found her voice.

"Ah, it's been fifty years..." He savored the moment as he leaned back in his chair.

"I know, Daddy."

"It's good to see you." His eyes softened as he gazed at me.

I wondered what was going on in his mind. Did I remind him of my mother? Was I anything like what he expected? Would he accept me as his child?

"Well, you probably have a lot of questions. What do you want to know?" Daddy asked.

"Tell me about yourself," I said.

"After I graduated from high school I enlisted in the army. I didn't want my mom to have to pay for me to go to college. She had four kids and didn't have money for that, so I decided to be a man and take care of myself."

"All right," I nodded my head in agreement.

"April 15, I went to Korea. There was a village named Nul No Ri that was a mile outside of the army base gate. That's where your mother lived. After a couple of weeks, a fellow soldier told me that he was being reassigned and he wanted to make sure his yobo was going to be taken care of."

"What's a yobo?"

"That's a live-in girlfriend."

"Ah, okay," I said.

"So that's when I met your mother. She was introduced to me as Judy, but her name was Chung Suk-ah." (The -ah suffix, which follows a Korean given name, is a sign of closeness, affection or a term of endearment.)

"So Judy is what the American soldier called her?"

"Yeah, that's what the Americans called her. I met her at her uncle's house. See, there were three teahouses in the village. But nobody was drinking tea in those houses." Daddy peered at me over the rim of his glasses.

"Oh? What were they drinking?"

"Well, they were bars, you see. Teahouse 1 was where the White boys went. Teahouse 2 was where you went if you wanted to get into trouble. That's where the Turks hung out. And Teahouse 3 was for the brothers."

"There were Turks there?"

"Yeah their base was a half mile away. You see, there were

no young Korean men in the village. They were all killed off in the Korean War, or they moved away. So there were just old men or very young boys."

"Mmmm, ok," I said.

"I befriended the KATUSA, Korean soldiers in the US Army, and learned how to speak Korean. They were stationed at the same army base, and they helped the US as allies. Those were some cool dudes. I learned how to read and write Korean from them. Nul No Ri is a two-and-a-half-hour drive north of Seoul, and that's where the army camp was."

"I tried to look that up when Nick gave me the name of the village, but I couldn't locate it on Google Maps," I said.

"Oh really? Let's see...there was a city, Munsan-ni, that was close by. And Libby Bridge wasn't too far. Uijeongbu village was also not far from Nul No Ri." (The village of Uijeongbu was the backdrop for the long-running American television show M*A*S*H.)

"Okay, I'll look again," I said.

"There's a river that separates North and South Korea, and we patrolled the DMZ south of the river. I spent nine years, six months, and twenty-two days in the army," Daddy said proudly.

"Your mom spoke English. She learned it from other people. But she couldn't read or write because she never went to school. Her parents were killed during the war. She lived with a family who kept her out of the bars, but she didn't go to the bars anyway because she didn't want to."

"Why didn't my mother go to school?"

"She was young when her parents died. And their school system in her village was not like what we are familiar with here in the US. We spent time—a lot of time—studying and translating English to Korean, and learning how to read. We were quite the pair. She was eager to learn, and I was eager to teach. Yeah, she was my first love. But the army didn't encourage marrying your yobo. You know what they told me?"

"What?"

"They told me, 'If the army would've wanted you to have a wife, we would've issued you one.' There was nothing I could do." Daddy shook his head. The anguish in his voice touched my heart.

"How old were you guys when you first met?"

"We were about eighteen years old. You know, funny thing, they told us not to drink the water, but it tasted so sweet that I drank as much water as I could! It was delicious!" I may have inherited his rebellious spirit.

"And the houses had an under-floor heating system," Daddy said.

"Oh? What was that like?"

"We took coal, you see, and put it in an inground firebox, and the heat from that was distributed underneath the floor. It heated up the whole room. It was pretty slick and worked really well."

"What was Mom like?"

"She smiled a lot. Well, at least she always smiled when she saw me." Daddy's cheeky grin made me laugh. "She was always happy. Curious as hell. She wanted to know about America and how things worked. She had lots of questions. She was fascinated by the typewriter. I was an assistant orderly room clerk and I wrote the passes for the soldiers to go off base. I wrote myself a pass every day to go see your mom when I got off work."

"That's how you got to spend so much time with her."

"That's right! I fell in the rice paddies twice trying to get back to the base before 11:00 p.m. curfew! I also had a Jeep accident trying to get back to Chung Suk-ah. I had just made a run to the airport, and I was driving too fast on those dirt roads. Nearly wiped out! Your mom was very feminine. Skinny as a rail. She tiptoed when she walked…walked on the balls of her feet. But she didn't wrap her feet like some of the other women in the village. She had normal feet."

I wondered if my mother's Korean neighbors borrowed the centuries-old Chinese tradition of foot binding. Girls aged four to seven had their arches and toes broken and bound by bandages to the soles of their feet. Once the feet healed, they repeated the breaking and wrapping process multiple times throughout the years as the girls grew into women. The goal being to modify the shape and size of the foot, making it smaller and more attractive to men. Mothers taught their daughters that the pain was necessary to gain the favor of an affluent suitor, increasing their chances of marrying into wealth. Others believed the procedure groomed women to work in jobs, like sewing, which required them to be immobile for lengthy periods of time. Those occupations were better suited for foot-bound women since manual field labor caused a great deal of podiatric pain. Foreigners who learned about the practice began a crusade to shed light on the oppressive ritual and the golden lotus feet, as they were called, were outlawed in China in 1912, although the custom was still practiced well into the mid twentieth century.

"How tall was she?"

Daddy's hand rubbed his chin as he looked up, as if to reach fifty years back in his memory bank to produce the answer. "About 4'11"–5'2"."

"That's a wide range. How tall are you, Daddy?"

"I'd say I'm 5'9". We had a wonderful relationship. We used to go for walks. I couldn't give her money because they weren't allowed to have American money. But I could go to the store and buy food or things that she needed for the house.

"Well, then she got pregnant. I had to leave because my tour was only for a year. I knew you were supposed to be born in July or August. We had a photographer friend who knew how to speak English. He would translate the letters that your mom would write to my mom, Sylvia."

"My mom wrote your mom letters?"

"She wrote three or four letters to your grandma. I sent

Sylvia some pictures of me and your mom that our photographer friend took. You can have the originals."

I paused. "You still have the pictures?"

"Oh yes, sweetheart! I have a picture of you and your mother too. I'll mail them to you."

"Wow…Daddy, I appreciate that. I'd like to see them right away. Can you text them to me?" I had waited my whole entire life for that opportunity. I didn't want to risk them getting lost in the mail.

"Sure, sure. I can do that when we hang up. I saw you in pictures, but I never met you in person. After you were a year to a year-and-a-half old, the letters stopped coming." Daddy's head and shoulders drooped slightly as a solemn look crept over his face.

"Why do you think that was? Did she die, get married, or something like that?"

"I don't know, sweetheart. Drove your grandma Sylvia crazy. She kept telling me, 'Find your daughter. Bring your Korean daughter to the US.' As a matter of fact, she went to the Korean consulate in New York multiple times to try to get help. But no one would help us find you."

My biological grandmother wanted to have a relationship with me. How endearing! She fought to try to find me, the foreign granddaughter that she had only viewed from afar, through photographs and grammatically incorrect English letters penned by a nonnative speaker. Little did she know, I ended up moving to the US when I was seven years old.

Daddy continued, "When I was eight years old, my mother moved to New York to find work and left me and my siblings in Barbados to live with her mother, your great-grandma Tanty. My mother became a nurse's aide and worked at Bellevue Hospital in Manhattan for thirty-four years. She was able to live in Manhattan, due to her job and her needing to be within a close proximity to the hospital. She would send back money and clothes for us."

"How many siblings do you have?"

"My mother had four children, but we were raised with another family in Barbados, like we are one family." Daddy brought his hands close to one another, forming a ball, indicating the cohesiveness of his nonconventional family.

"One of my brothers died of a heart attack at fifty years old. Happened in the subway, people were just stepping over him. His two daughters live in New York."

"Awww, that's sad."

"My other brother died from pneumonia in Boston in 1989. He was in his forties, but he drank a lot and lived a fast life. Fought all the time and was very defiant. And our baby sister, Candy, lives in New York with her husband and their two sons. The oldest lives in Grandma Sylvia's apartment in Manhattan."

Good thing Grandma's apartment was still in the family.

"He lived there when Sylvia was sick. Then me and my wife went up there to help take care of her until she died. She was an only child but always wanted siblings. She was pretty close to some cousins that we have who live in Canada. They are from Barbados too.

"Sylvia was like the mayor of 26th Street. She adopted everyone, and all loved her. Even when she was sick, she never complained."

"What was she sick with?"

"She had pancreatic cancer. She was diagnosed with it, and six months later, she was gone. She died in 2010."

"Sorry for your loss, Daddy."

"Eh, thank you. Her mother, your great-grandma Tanty, died of hypertension when she was ninety-four. That was back in 2002."

"Does hypertension run in the family?"

"Yes, and heart disease runs in the family too. Your grandma also had diabetes and was insulin dependent. Her father was insulin dependent and so is one of your brothers."

All good things to know. Adoptees who know nothing about their biological families know even less about their inherited genetic risk factors.

"Your grandma would be delighted that you found us. When your sister Diana found out about you, she said she was going to find you—for Grandma. Never did it ever occur to me that you were adopted. You were lost, baby girl, not abandoned."

Not only did my biological father know about me, his mother knew about me as well. I did my best to keep my emotions in check, but my facial filter was broken. It never worked well in the first place, but as I aged, the phrase 'it's written all over your face' increasingly applied to me, even when I didn't want it to.

"Thank you, Daddy. Will you please send me the pics of you and Mom?"

"I'll do that right now."

"I am so happy to meet you finally. After all of these years!" I said.

"Yes, well, it's never too late!"

As promised, Daddy texted me the pictures he had cherished for the past fifty years. My curiosity prevailed over emotion. A lifetime of wondering halted as I stared at the head and shoulders close-up of my umma, the Korean word for mother. She was as beautiful as I had imagined. Her black hair, pulled back into a bun, showcased a forehead and hairline like mine. Her fair skin looked flawless. Seeing her eyebrows, chin, and face shape was like viewing my own reflection in a mirror.

The next four pictures arrived upside down and were all of the same Christmas card. It read, "Merry Christmas Korea 1967," and it displayed a picture of Jesus with his disciples seated at the Last Supper. The upper middle portion of the card displayed the first picture that Daddy sent of my mother. I affixed an assiduous stare to the picture for an extended period, so grateful for that moment. I became emotional as I thanked God for hearing and answering my prayers. To see a picture of my mother, to know her name, to learn about her as an individual…to be able to speak with Daddy, to learn about my roots, my origins, my family history. Does anyone out there hear me when I say GOD IS GOOD?

The next picture took my breath away. My mother stood outside of her home, holding me in her arms. Judging from our attire and my age, it was springtime 1968. She guided my tiny hand as I shared food with her. Such a sweet, tender moment to capture on camera—the baby girl feeding her umma instead of umma feeding her.

Me and my mother in 1968

I know my umma loved me. I could *feel* it through that photograph. She took care of me for as long as she could, against insurmountable odds. Even to this day, unwed mothers are taboo in South Korea and are often excommunicated from the family. Social norms in the late 1960s and 1970s dictated that no Korean man would want to marry her, especially if she had a mixed-race child. Babies born out of wedlock could not be added to a family register if the father was not Korean or if no Korean man claimed the child as his own. If you were not on a family register, you were not a Korean citizen, which made you ineligible for government benefits and civic rights.

That stigma and resulting predicament all too often led women to leave their babies in public places, such as police, bus, and train stations or hospitals. Child abandonment was illegal, but desperate mothers knew that babies found on South Korean soil, by default, became Korean citizens. Women abandoned their precious bundles of joy, hoping they would be found by someone who could help them lead a life where they would not be treated like an outcast due to the circumstances surrounding their birth.

CHAPTER 7

Forever Family

I TOLD MY CHURCH congregation, during Sunday morning worship service, about how God had worked miracles in my life. The odds of finding my birth family, and them openly wanting a relationship with me, were slim. That was the second time that I had spoken publicly about my adoption, the first time being three years prior at my friend's Christmas party. Talking in front of large groups put me outside of my comfort zone, but I spoke of God's goodness to give hope to others. After the service ended, church members hugged me a little tighter as they congratulated me and wished me well with God's continued blessings over my life. I loved my church family, many of whom I'd known for over twenty years. We'd overcome substantial challenges together and had grown individually, collectively, and spiritually in the process.

After church, I arrived at my parents' house carrying two take-and-bake pizzas. I greeted them with hugs and kisses before walking into the kitchen to put our dinner in the oven. James showed up not long after. He and I always drove separately to church on Sunday mornings. His trustee and treasurer duties required him to stay after worship service ended to count donations and facilitate bank deposits.

I walked into the living room and sat next to my mom on the couch. Quiet-natured and nurturing, my adoptive mother did not let her 4'10" stature limit her occasional sassiness. A stay-at-home mom by trade, she had dinner on the table by 5:00 p.m. every evening. My two older brothers and I benefited from having her at home after school and during the summer months; thus, we never had to experience day care or babysitters. That upbringing instilled a desire in me to make sure my own children didn't have to attend day care. James and I made the decision to work opposite shifts so our kids would have one parent with them for most of the day and night.

My mother had experienced a lot in her eighty-seven years on this earth. Born during the Great Depression era, her childhood home didn't have indoor plumbing or electricity. She witnessed the US enter World War II when she was a young girl and grew up to serve as a military wife during the Vietnam War. She raised her children during the civil rights movement and lived to see a Black man get elected to the White House, twice. Her eighth-grade education laid the foundation for her success with taking the General Educational Development (GED) test while in her fifties. Introduction to the digital age later in life posed no problem for her. Playing slot machines on the computer was one of her favorite pastimes.

Mom taught me to be self-sufficient, confident, God-fearing, and independent. She grew up in an era when women did not work outside of the home, and the man of the household ruled the roost. She didn't want me to have to depend on a man to take care of me—she raised me to be my own person.

She gave me advice when friends and boys weren't acting the way I thought they should. Countless times I cried on her shoulder when peers talked about me. She'd say, 'they talked about Jesus. What makes you better than Him?' Good point.

My mother disciplined me when needed, encouraged high

scholastic achievement, and was a tremendous help when my children were born. She loved me as if I had grown inside of her womb.

"Hey, you got your projector out," I observed. Round Kodak carousels holding our family's memories from the 1960s and 1970s were stacked neatly in a box next to the dining room table.

"Yeah, I'd like to look through some old slides. I found the ones from my tours in Okinawa and England." Dad walked over to grab a carousel. Satisfied with the one he'd chosen, he settled back down into his favorite rocker-recliner.

"That's when Clayton and Miles were little boys," I said.

"Yeah, and that's when we got you." Mom smiled.

"It's interesting that you say that. I have some amazing news. I found my biological father." No sense in wasting that segue or beating around the bush.

"What?" said Mom. Both parents stared in my direction.

"I found my biological father, and some siblings. I took a DNA test and my brother came back as a match." My rapid blinking was almost in sync with my heart rate as I examined my parents' expressions.

Mom's eyes widened as her hands raised to touch her face. "Oh, that's wonderful! Congratulations!"

"Wow, that's a one-in-a-million chance." Dad's bushy eyebrows lifted as he looked at me. He brought his fingertips together, forming a pyramid of sorts across his lap.

"I know, it's crazy." My darting gaze found rest when it met my mother's face.

"Your dad is still alive?" she asked.

"Yes. I spoke with him two days ago. He knew about me, and he said he had a relationship with my mom. He knew she was pregnant when he got reassigned to Okinawa, but he couldn't take her with him. He lost touch with her and he didn't know what happened to me. He assumed I was raised by my mother."

"Nah, that would have been hard for your mother. Raising a mixed child—the Korean society would have made that difficult," Dad said.

"Yeah, I know."

"Is your mom still alive?" Mom asked.

"I don't know, I'm still looking for her. The Ancestry test didn't return any matches on my maternal side. My brother was the only one who responded to my message on my paternal side."

"Did the test say he was your brother?" Dad leaned forward in his recliner.

"When you look at how many DNA segments we matched on, it put us in the half sibling range, but I guess it didn't specifically declare us brother and sister." I glanced at James, who gave me a slight nod.

"Have you spoken to your brother?" asked Mom.

"Yes, James and I had a conversation with him and his wife this past Thursday. He told me that I was their oldest sister, and that I was the first of seven. In total, there are four girls and three boys."

"You have sisters." Mom giggled.

"I know! I've always wanted one of those!" The energy of my words permeated the room.

"When we first moved into our house forty-one years ago, one of the neighbor girls asked me, 'Where are the others?' I didn't know who she was talking about. You told her you had some sisters, and she wanted to know where they were." That sounded like something my nine-year-old self would have said.

"That's amazing that you found your father. A lot of men deny their kids because they don't want their families knowing what they were doing back then," Dad said.

"I can see that. Daddy said that the army didn't encourage them to marry their girlfriends. He said his superior officer told him that if the army wanted him to have a wife, they would have issued him one."

"The air force wouldn't have done that. They wanted families to stay together. There were plenty of airmen who had babies with women overseas, and they were allowed to marry," Dad said.

Interracial marriage became legal in the United States in 1967, dismantling centuries-old miscegenation laws. While it was legal in some states prior to that year, sixteen states still had laws on the books forbidding the practice when the Supreme Court ruling was handed down. Even after the legal mandates, some states were slow to repeal laws that made interracial marriage a felony. Alabama didn't amend its state constitution until the new millennium hit in the year 2000.

Dad repositioned his glasses higher on the bridge of his nose. "Ancestry didn't say that he was your father?" Parental advice followed Dad's rhetorical question, whether I wanted it or not. "The thing to do would be to take a paternity test. That way there's no question and there won't be any confusion. You'll know for sure. It'd be a shame for you to establish a relationship and discover he's not your father. I just don't want you to get hurt."

My dad was *always* right in his own mind. He argued against the Encyclopedia Britannica. I never liked to admit when he was right, but in that instance, I knew his reasoning came from a place of love and concern.

"Yeah, that does make a lot of sense. I'll ask him if he is willing to take a test. It would put my mind at ease," I said.

"It's best to be sure. If he's really your father, you beat the odds. I'm really happy for you. I hope it works out. I guess you'll have two dads." A reassuring smile accompanied his hand steeple as he rocked back and forth in his chair. Two dads? Handling one growing up was enough of a challenge.

"Thank you both for raising me and giving me a forever home. There are so many orphans who aren't that fortunate. Some age out of the system and find themselves without any family and surviving on their own once they hit their late teens.

I thank you for loving me."

My eyes softened as I smiled and reached to cup Mom's hand in my own.

"You're very welcome, sweetheart," Mom said.

"Aw, you're welcome," Dad said.

"My sister Diana and Daddy wanted me to thank you on their behalf as well. Daddy said that his mother, my grandmother, went to the Korean consulate multiple times trying to get help finding me."

"Is she still alive?" Mom asked.

"No, she died in 2010. Diana said that after Grandma passed away she prayed that I was ok, and that she wanted to find me for Grandma's sake. My mom is from a village two and a half hours north of Seoul, near the DMZ."

"The orphanage was two hours north of Seoul," Dad said.

That was news to me. "I thought it was in Seoul." The expression on my face changed.

"No, they flew us into Seoul to spend the day with the child that we were going to adopt, but the little girl that we selected knew her mother, and she didn't want to go," Dad said. "Since we were already there, the chaplain asked the orphanage director if there were any more girls who were ready for adoption. We had to wait at the hotel until they brought you to us later that day. You didn't want anything to do with me, you just clung to your mother." It was a good thing Dad found that humorous. The corners of Mom's mouth turned up as her smile stretched wide across her face.

I didn't realize it before, but the orphanage wasn't located in Seoul, the adoption agency was. The picture was starting to become clearer. The blank canvas of my early childhood started to gain abstract spots of color. My mother's village, toward the top of the masterpiece, was sprinkled with yellow and brown droplets with swirls of red connecting them. The blue river flowed south toward the orphanage. The last place where I would feel my umma's touch.

MY ADOPTIVE BROTHER CLAYTON, ten years my senior, moved out of the house when I was seven years old and enlisted in the navy. After serving sixteen years in the military, he moved to Omaha to live closer to family. I helped him get hired at the Fortune 500 tech company I worked for at the time, and after a few years, his business unit relocated to Georgia, where he has lived ever since with his wife.

His only child was born on my thirteenth birthday. I tried to return the favor with my first born, but Capris entered the world the day after her Uncle Clayton's thirty-seventh birthday. My personalized car license plate read RUNNL8. Being on time had always been a challenge in my adult life. It's a skill that I'd worked hard to improve.

"Hello?" Hearing my brother's voice made me smile.

"Hey, Clayton, what are you up to?"

"Just got home from work and getting ready to get something to eat. What are you doing?"

"I have big news."

"Oh yeah? What's that?"

"I found my birth father." I was amazed those true words rolled off my tongue with surety.

"You found your what?" His tone beckoned for clarity.

"I found my biological dad through Ancestry DNA."

"Oh wow, CONGRATUALTIONS!"

"He's still alive and lives in Illinois. And you know what else is crazy?"

"What?"

"I'm the oldest of seven!" I sat in my cuddle chair in my bedroom, picturing the expression on my oldest brother's face.

"What? Oh wow…" Clayton continued after a brief pause, "Well, it serves you right!" We both laughed at his teasing.

"I'm pretty sure my baby sister is nowhere near as bratty as

I was growing up, so I think I'm good!" My annoying tendencies as a young girl came to mind.

"You weren't that bratty. Oh wow, that's great. I'm happy for you!"

I recounted the last thirty-six hours and filled him in on who's who, who's where, and how the revelation had been uncovered.

"The way I see it, I just gained six new little brothers and sisters," Clayton said. He always did have a generous and compassionate heart. He once told me that there were only a few people he would take a bullet for in this world, and I was one of them. I never understood how much my love for my brother was reciprocated until he told me that.

MY ADOPTIVE BROTHER MILES was five years older than me, but not much taller. He's the sibling I grew up with since Clayton moved out when I was still young. He sported a sizeable afro in the 1970s, which gave way to a shag haircut in the 1980s. His passion for fashion and photography often led to me posing as the model for his photo shoots. He styled me in Jordache, Sasson, or Sergio Valente jeans paired with a popped collar shirt or a matching denim jacket. My big hair and I could have stepped off the pages of a magazine. I wish I knew where those priceless pictures were. Those photo shoots sparked short-lived aspirations of a modeling career that I would never pursue. Miles spent countless hours in the darkroom at the high school developing 35mm film for school projects, the yearbook, and friends and family photo albums.

Although his condition went undiagnosed, I am certain he suffered from dyslexia. Difficulty reading contributed to poor grades in school, which led to other challenges. Later in life, he was diagnosed with bipolar disorder. My father found him in his apartment in the spring of 2007, deceased from an enlarged heart. His sudden death, at forty-four years old was a shock for all of us.

I would never be able to tell him about my birth family. He and I never discussed them. What he would think? What advice he would give me? I didn't always listen to his opinions, but I would have loved to share this news with him.

CHAPTER 8

Sibling Conversations

I RECEIVED MY FIRST text from my younger brother a couple of hours after my phone conversation with Daddy.

Text Message
Fri, Jan 19, 6:29 PM

Hey, this is Rob.

Thanks for texting! I'll add you to my contacts.

I've got a bit of time before I have to get ready for work, did you want to talk for a bit?

Yes!

"Hi, Rob! I'm glad to meet you officially, even if it is via phone." I loved hearing my newfound brother's voice for the first time. Not wanting to freak him out by being overly excited, I toned it down.

"You know I had to Google you, right?"

I laughed as I said, "Oh really?"

"I've got some strange woman messaging me saying she's my long-lost sister—of course I had to Google you."

"Well, of course!" I raised one eyebrow. A slow wide grin stretched across my face. "Oh boy, what did you see? The picture that probably comes up is a horrible one. We had to take them for work, and it's awful, I hate it."

"Why do you hate it?"

"It's not my best pose. But I hate taking pictures anyway. I'm not photogenic." I didn't mind my brother Miles using me as a model when I was a teenager, but I quickly discovered the camera didn't always love me.

"That's not what I saw."

"Hmmm, what'd you see?"

"*Family Feud?*" Rob didn't suppress his amusement.

Laughter erupted. "Oh no! Our audition video?"

"Oh yes!" Rob rubbed his hands together.

"Oh my gosh, that's so embarrassing!"

"I thought it was funny!"

"Ha! Interesting story. The producers were in Omaha, but we missed them because James doesn't check his email on a regular basis. They responded to our request for an audition, but only sent the reply to James. He didn't read that email until after they left town."

When James fessed up and told us he got the message, I told him he should have taken that information to his grave. I would have never told the rest of the group. But his sisters inquired about the next closest audition city. We found out the show's producers were going to be in Chicago. We took a road trip and attended Capris's volleyball match Friday night at Loyola, went to the audition in Chicago on Saturday morning, then drove to Peoria to watch her team play against Bradley Saturday night.

Besides James and me, our team included his two sisters and his brother-in-law. The show flew us to Atlanta for three days and two nights. My brother Clayton and his wife, along with James's son Chris, and his wife, got to come to the studio on the first day to be part of the audience. Unfortunately, we didn't get to compete that day. Our family wasn't in the audience on the second day, when we made it on stage, so no one knew how we fared. We made everyone wait until the show aired five months later to reveal the outcome.

"How'd you do?" asked Rob.

"We played against three families, won two of the games, and came out victorious in the second fast money round. It was a blast, but man, it was stressful."

Our two days at the Atlanta Convention Center, where the episodes were recorded, began at 7:00 a.m. and ended around 7:30 p.m. when the van driver dropped us off at our hotel.

One of the most agonizing things about the whole experience was the uncertainty of getting on stage. Even though families made it through auditions in their home cities, teams had to fight for a spot on stage after arriving at the studio. It was like auditioning all over again. While waiting in the green room, we heard stories of families who had come from across the country, waited in that same room for two whole days, then returned home without ever getting to compete on camera, in front of the live studio audience. We did not want that to become our fate.

The show's producers always expected each family member to exude an elevated level of energy—more difficult to do than it sounds. It's abnormal to be that bubbly for such an extended period, but we smiled, bounced, cheered, and otherwise acted out of character every time we sensed someone important was watching.

The TV show staff instructed us to enunciate our words and speak loud enough to be heard in the next room. Of course, all those instructions fell by the wayside once we were in the heat of competition.

Steve Harvey, the host, interacted with the studio audience during recording breaks and was very down-to-earth and entertaining. The production staff was super helpful and encouraging. They really wanted you to win. But the producer kept yelling at us. She didn't like the answers we were giving; she told us we were too smart for our own good and to dumb it down. She said it was child's play and we were making it way too difficult. Then she marched over to our opponent and told them that we were giving them the game, but they weren't taking it! I suppose she meant well and was trying to fuel our competitive edge.

In the first game, we were three points shy of winning the fast money round. Right before the second fast money round, the producer came backstage while I was preparing to put on soundproof earphones so I couldn't hear the answers my brother-in-law was about to give. She sternly told me to go out and win for my family. I put my game face on, and we ended up triumphant. I'm glad we did it. That was one of my bucket list items.

"Cool, cool," said Rob. "So what do you want to know about the family?"

"Whatever you want to tell me."

"To start, Dad ran a business in Germany, and my mom did the books; that's how they met. Our brother Anthony's mom had a hard time with her parents after becoming pregnant with a Black child. They gave her a lower position in the family, I guess. That might have been part of the reason why she sent him back to Germany when he was twelve. I've only seen Anthony three times in person."

My brother's statement surprised me.

"Nadine and I were raised by our mom after she and Dad got divorced. I went to Dad's house a handful of times as a kid, but he never did anything to raise me. In my opinion, it's the parent's responsibility to care for the family."

"Yes, I agree," I said.

"He just wasn't there for me and Nadine like that. But she's always loved him. She's more forgiving in that regard. The last time I spoke to Nick was when I worked as a bouncer at a bar. He was in there with some buddies celebrating someone's twenty-first birthday. And that was probably ten years ago."

It was becoming evident that not all of my siblings interacted with each other on a regular basis.

"I met Devin once. Probably when I met Diana last year."

"Really? And you and Devin grew up in the same city?"

"Yep."

"Okay," I said. "So tell me about your interests, and your family."

"I've worked a lot of odd jobs…bouncer, bartender. I enrolled in a music occupation program. I taught music lessons for a while, taught ballroom dancing, played in a band." Great-grandfather's entertainer gene was thriving.

"What instrument do you play?"

"Piano."

"I love the piano, and I always wanted to play. I took lessons for years, but I can't read music. I memorized one song that I used to play, but it's been so long."

"You can pick it back up." Rob's encouragement would have given me hope if I hadn't already discovered that playing an instrument was not my calling.

"No, that's not my gift. I love to sing too, but I'm not all that great at that either, so maybe you can teach me?"

"I might have some suggestions that will help you."

"That'd be awesome! So your family—married, kids?"

"I got married six years ago. My stepdaughter is a junior in high school."

"I'd like to meet everyone. I'm thinking about planning a trip."

"Oh yeah? When are you thinking?"

"Soon. What does your February look like?"

"My days off rotate, and I don't get very many weekends off. Let's see, I'm off February 17 and 18 and 24 and 25."

"I already have an out-of-town trip scheduled on February

18, so that might not work. But the 24 and 25 look good. I just need to check with James and my girls to see if that works for them. I'll also check with Nick and maybe we can meet them as well."

Elated doesn't even come close to describing the euphoric aura that engulfed me when I thought about meeting my family, sharing the same space, and breathing the same oxygen as them. It gave my life meaning and purpose. I was destined to find them.

I ASKED JAMES IF he wanted to join me on a video chat with Devin and Nick.

"Hello hello?" My brother greeted us as his oldest daughter, Alexandria, sat on his lap. Her shy smile and bouncy curls grabbed my heart and burrowed in deep. Devin sat next to our brother at the kitchen breakfast bar. We caught a glimpse of superhero Gideon dashing by in the background.

"Hello!" All my teeth were showing as I smiled wide.

"Hey, what's up?" said James. That was so surreal for me. Interacting with blood relatives. Siblings I never knew I had. Nieces and nephews who were unknown to me. We started right in as if we had known each other all of our lives.

"Devin, how was your flight?' I asked. Her sewn-in braids were long enough to reach her waist.

"It was good. All of the flights were on time, so nothing too crazy."

Nick's wife, Anna-Marie, popped her head in. "Hey!" She rocked a big smile and a super cute GI Jane buzz cut. I imagine having less hair to manage must simplify the daily routine of a mother whose four kids were all three years old or younger.

"Well, hello there! Congrats again on your new baby!" I said. Right on cue, Anna-Marie's mom appeared with baby Marcus, tilting him toward the camera.

"Anna-Marie's mother is staying with us for a few weeks," Nick said.

"Are you from out of town?" James asked.

"California," she replied.

"You're there helping with the baby?"

As she nodded, Nick introduced us to his mother, who came into camera view holding Olivia.

"Hello," she said with a quick wave. "Nice to meet you. I've heard a lot about you."

"Nice to meet you too!" I shifted my gaze to Nick. "Looks like you have a lot of help. You brought in the professionals!"

He laughed before saying, "They're a big help. It's nice having someone here so I don't have to bundle all of the kids up when I take the older two to preschool."

"That's a big help. Ours didn't like wearing their winter coats when they were young. Sometimes we'd have to chase them down just to get it on them," James said.

"How are you doing, Miss Alexandria?" I asked. Her shy smile resurfaced. "Did you go to school today?" She nodded her head. "What did you do at school?"

"I made a card for Auntie Devin." She twisted her index finger in her mouth.

"You did? What type of card?" I asked.

"It's gonna be for Valentine's Day."

"That's nice, I bet she will love that."

"It's pink with hearts. I wrote my name on the back."

"Do they call you Alex at school?"

"Who?" Alexandria looked confused by my question.

"Your friends or teachers. Do they call you Alex?"

"No."

"Does anyone call you Alex, or do you have a different nickname?" I asked.

"No, but sometimes…" Alexandria brought her three-year-old face close to the camera. "Grandmother calls me George." Laughter exploded from all within earshot.

"Hey, big man, you ready for bed?" Nick asked Gideon. He said no as he ran by, but Anna-Marie corralled him and whisked him away to his superhero cave, otherwise known as his bedroom.

"Go find Mommy, it's getting close to bedtime," Nick said to Alexandria.

"Good night, Alexandria, it was nice talking to you," I said.

There were smooches all around and then bouncy curls disappeared out of sight.

"Your kids are soooo cute!" I told my brother.

"Ah, thanks. They're a lot of fun. It's nice that I can be here with them while Anna-Marie goes to school."

"James and I always worked opposite schedules when our girls were young so they didn't have to spend much time in day care. Hey, I just got off a call with Rob."

"Oh yeah?" said Nick.

"Yep. We were talking about dates for a road trip so we could come meet you guys."

"Nice! When are you thinking?" Nick asked.

"He doesn't have very many weekends off, but he's free February 24 and 25. How far are you from Daddy?"

"About two and a half hours."

"Is that all?" James replied.

"If that's the case, maybe we can drive to Chicago on the 23rd, then drive to Peoria on the 24th," I said.

"I'll look at flights and I'll try to come back that weekend. I'm already coming back home for spring break in April, but I'll see how much it is," Devin said.

"That would be awesome! I'd love to meet everyone."

"So Li, how did you and James meet?" Nick asked.

"We met at a Keith Sweat concert," I said.

"I saw this cute little thang with long black hair walk past me wearing a little black mini skirt," said James.

"Oh nice," said Nick. His laugh indicated he knew there was more to the story.

James had been standing at the base of the stairs that led to the second floor of the Civic Auditorium Arena in Omaha. My friend and I were leaning against a table, facing the crowded lobby. James had looked in our direction, then raised his hand in front of him and motioned for me to come. I turned around to see nothing but a wall behind me. I looked back in his direction and put my hand to my chest and mouthed, "Me?" I would have been embarrassed to walk all the way across the room if he hadn't been motioning to me.

When the intermission ended, we went back in the auditorium. I stood on the seat of a chair to get a better view of the band. James stood in front of me.

"She was rubbing her hands all over my chest," James said.

"I WAS NOT." I had rested my hands on his shoulders to brace myself. His hands had found my bare legs.

"The girl's got some big ole calves!" I didn't know at the time James thought they were sexy.

Nick and Devin laughed. We spent the rest of the time learning more about each other's immediate families and discussing our backgrounds. Nick and Devin shared a close sibling bond. They lived thousands of miles away from each other, but they communicated daily and had a good grasp of the happenings in each other's world. It was also evident their lives were family-centered and faith-based.

After our FaceTime with them, James and I tracked down Capris and Candace.

"I have exciting news! Remember a few weeks ago when I told you I had taken some DNA tests?"

"Yeah." My daughters responded in unison.

"I got the results back. My beliefs about my ethnicity were confirmed, but the interesting thing is I found my birth family on my father's side."

"Wow!"

"What?"

"I've only gotten the Ancestry DNA test results back, but

it matched me with my brother. He lives in Chicago with his family. Your dad and I spoke with him and his wife yesterday."

"No way!" exclaimed Capris.

"That's cool!" said Candace.

"Yeah, and you know what else is crazy?" I said.

"What?"

"I'm the oldest of seven!" Excited laughter and a feeling of disbelief engulfed me.

"Wow, I'm truly happy for you, Mom," said Capris.

Candace echoed her sentiment. "Yeah, that is awesome."

"I'd like to plan a trip to meet everyone," I said.

We spent several minutes discussing the family and potential travel plans. "I'll check on these details and let you know. You guys, this is so crazy. Now you have real aunties and uncles instead of just play ones—otherwise known as your parents' friends," I said as we all laughed.

"That's right, and you have little cousins that you get to meet," James said.

"I can't wait!" said Candace.

"I'm looking forward to it, that's so awesome!" said Capris.

"Candace, your uncle Nick said he was going to be a pharmacist until he didn't do so well in a chemistry class, so he figured he should do something else," James said.

"Yeah, it's hard!" Candace replied.

"And your auntie Devin was a thrower in college. I guess that runs in the family, with you being a thrower on your high school track team, Simonie. She also played volleyball, and coaches at the middle school where she teaches," I said.

"I guess that runs in the family too," said Capris.

"We have lots to discover about our newfound family. I'm so excited to get to know them. It's getting late. Simonie, I'll find out about the flights, and we'll firm up the travel plans here pretty quick," I said.

James sat across from me and grabbed my hand. This blessing was so unexpected. So marvelous. So miraculous.

THE NEXT MORNING, I shared my excitement with Diana.

> Jan 20, 2018
>
> I had a fantastic conversation with Dad! I love him 💘
>
> 6:36 AM ✓✓

Diana: "I know you do. I know. Yeah, he was very emotional. He wrote me a WhatsApp this morning too. Everybody is six hours behind me, or seven hours. It's so not fair. And Robert told me he thinks you're a great personality and a lovely woman and he can't wait to meet you. Oh my god, I want to meet you too! Well, I'm trying to get there, as I said, in July. My ex-husband is an ex-military soldier; he has post-traumatic stress. He's in the States somewhere, I don't know where, but his mother is in Houston. My daughter turns twelve and I can't stop her from meeting her dad. And I think she's stable enough in case he has any depression or drama in that time. I promised her to be in the country while she's at her grandma's. We're coming in July and probably going to stay at Dad's house or at Nick's house, or my friend lives in Chicago. My fiancé's sister lives in Kentucky. Maybe we can hug then. What do you think? And isn't his voice great? I love Dad's voice, I love it. He has such a big heart. I'm telling you, he's a crazy guy, he's really insane, and he does know. Ha! But that makes him so sweet."

Li: "Yes, this summer will be perfect. There will be lots of hugs and fun. My adoptive parents are from Kentucky and we have quite a bit of family there in Louisville, Lexington, and a little town called Hazard, which is roughly two hours away from Lexington. I have fond memories of Kentucky because I used to spend summers there. So as you're making your rounds in the US, you can stop by Omaha. We've got plenty of room for you to stay with us. And then maybe we could go to Chicago together, or I'll meet you in Chicago. Let me know where your plans take you and I'll be there. Ok?"

Diana: "Sure! Did you tell your daughters and your adoptive parents? And how do you feel? Do you feel good? Does it give you energy? 'Cause I'm floated with energy. I finally feel that family on my dad's side now is complete. Because Grandma told me so much about her pain because of her grandkids and stuff. And after she passed away it feels like she keeps talking to me. I know it sounds crazy, but sometimes I feel her pain. So I'm very relaxed now, and I feel relief, and I think she's happy now. Finally, she's happy."

Li: "I am elated as well. I am very humbled…and thankful to God for allowing that to happen the way it did. I understand what you mean when you say that you can still feel Grandma's pain. I get that. So yes, I was able to talk to both girls last night and told them the whole story. They were amazed and excited and can't wait to meet everyone. They're very happy for me because they know this has been a journey. They're eager to learn about their family and to meet their blood relatives. It's thrilling for all of us."

CHAPTER 9

Meeting Face-to-Face

I FACETIMED WITH NICK to finalize our plans a week prior to the trip.

"We'll hang out with you guys on Friday, then head to Peoria on Saturday," I said.

"Cool. Me, Anna-Marie, and the kids are going to go to Peoria too."

"That's awesome!"

"I reached out to Nadine, and she said you all were planning on going to dinner. If it's ok, I think we'll join you."

"That would be amazing!" Hanging out with multiple siblings at the same time, getting to know them and their families, savoring those moments with my own blood relatives—all blessings beyond measure.

James and I got a 6:00 a.m. start on the morning of February 23. Two hours into our road trip, we met Capris at a gas station along Interstate 80. I joined her in her car as James followed us in mine.

One-on-one windshield time with my girls is the best. They're my biggest fans and my sharpest critics. They keep me grounded with love, respect, and honesty.

Capris and I find humor in the same things, and we both love to laugh. We're easygoing and down-to-earth. We say the same things at the exact same time, with the same voice intonation. And we are keeping a running tally of the bad traits she inherited from me. Things like tears flowing from our eyes when we laugh, adult acne, and not being to tame the stray strands of hair that frame our faces or protrude from the top of our heads. We are up to 108 traits.

Candace despises ground meat, good morning texts, and small talk, and she's the number one source of entertainment in the family. The things she says and does keep all of us in stitches. When she was in middle school, she went through a phase where she quoted internet memes, and none of us knew what she was saying or why. She finally showed us the YouTube videos and clued us in to what we had been hearing daily for months. We laughed until we cried. She is unwavering in her beliefs, passionate about fighting social injustice, and compassionate toward animals and the elderly.

Until that day, my daughters were the only blood relatives I had been face-to-face with. Now, by God's predetermined grace, I was going to meet additional biological family members for the first time. The excitement made my heart race with anticipation.

I checked in with Nick to give him a trip progress report when we stopped for lunch.

> Well we just got back on the road because we took an extended break which included ukulele lessons 😑. We are 155 miles from Chicago

> Lol I mean that's a good enough reason

> No rush

"So this is the big weekend. How are you feeling?" Capris asked me as she parallel parked next to the curb in front of

Nick's house. The 3:30 p.m. sun hid behind clouds in the overcast sky in this quiet suburban neighborhood with winding streets.

"I'm feeling fantastic. Excited." A smile stretched across my face as I folded my winter scarf before tossing it gently onto the back seat.

"Oh my gosh" slipped from my lips as I proceeded up the paved walkway toward the front door. My niece Alexandria stood in the doorway with her daddy Nick at her side. I met their smiles with a big one of my own.

"Hello!" I said just as Nick opened the door. Anna-Marie stood behind Alexandria and encouraged her to say hi; she gave us a tiny wave and a smile, then grabbed on to her daddy's leg like a security blanket.

"Hello, come on in, come on in," said Nick as he opened the door wider to allow for our entry. His outstretched arm found its way around my shoulders to envelope me into a heartfelt hug. His 6'1" athletic physique was strong and comforting. Our prolonged embrace was filled with reassurance that I had found my biological family and that they would be with me until we were called to depart this earthly vessel. I closed my eyes tight as I rested my head on his chest. The world stopped rotating. My brain was empty. No thoughts raced through my mind. I stood there and lived in that moment. My emotions remained intact until Nick took a deep sigh during our embrace. I detected his sniffle, which triggered my own tears.

I was thankful Nick had responded to my initial inquiry. Appreciative of my brother's invitation to visit. Grateful for God's grace, mercy, and favor.

We pulled apart from our hug and held hands while facing each other. Standing there looking into my brother's eyes was so surreal. Our smiles gave way to gentle laughter.

"Come see my baby brother." Alexandria grabbed Capris's hand and led the way into the dining room where one-month-old Marcus slumbered in a newborn baby nest. A Carolina blue baby blanket adorned with gray and white elephants and his monogramed name had been draped over him.

My precious nephew would never know a time when Auntie Li was not around.

"Wanna see our playroom?" My niece beckoned for us to follow her into every kid's dream toy room. Glass patio doors on the west side of the large room opened to the fenced-in, tree-shaded backyard. The large sectional sofa on the east side of the room tripled as a trampoline and private fort when couch cushions and blankets were arranged to erect a secret hideaway. Various building blocks, action figures, superhero costumes, and other toys instrumental in igniting young imaginations were sprinkled across the floor. Alexandria walked over to a kitchen toy set, tucked behind the sofa, and whipped up her specialty of the day. It was delicious, of course, and we let her know how much we loved her menu choice.

Soft coos drew me back into the dining room. Anna-Marie must have sensed my eagerness to hold Marcus, so she handed me a small baby blanket.

"He spits up a lot, so you might want to put this over your shoulder."

After I washed my hands, newborn baby scent accompanied her bundle of joy into my arms. I bouncy walked with him for a few minutes before settling down into a kitchen chair. He rested his head on my shoulder.

My nephew, Gideon, woke up from his nap. He and Uncle James became instant buddies. They found their way to the piano situated between the open kitchen and dining room. The two collaborated on a musical masterpiece that won't ever be ready for a public performance. Story time with Uncle James was next on the agenda. Alexandria and Gideon sat next to him on the deep brown leather bench at the dining room table.

Marcus drifted back into infant slumberland with his tiny head snuggled into my neck. I answered my ringing phone.

"Hey, Simonie, are you here?"

"Liza! I just landed," said Candace.

"We'll start heading that way. Let us know which door you exit."

"I have to go to baggage claim and I'll text you once I get down there."

"Sounds good, sweetie. See you in a bit. Love you."

"Love you too!"

"Nick, Candace's plane just landed and she's ready to be picked up."

"Ok, cool. Let me finish up, then I'll grab my keys and we can head out." Nick put away the extra avocados he hadn't used for the guacamole he made.

I transferred my sweet sleeping nephew back into his baby nest. "Candace's flight landed. Do you want to go with me and Nick to pick her up?" I interrupted story time.

"Sure, I'll go." James informed Alexandria and Gideon that he needed to go pick up their other cousin.

Chicago O'Hare International Airport was a twenty-minute drive from my brother's house. We swooped Candace up and were back home before we knew it. Since we had left our luggage in the car earlier, we brought our bags into the house upon our return.

I emerged from the basement, where we'd be staying, with a paper sack full of novelty presents for my newly discovered family. Personalized artwork for Nick, a silver bracelet made from my handwriting for Anna-Marie, a monogramed chef hat and apron for Alexandria, a dinosaur mask and cape for Gideon, and a little stuffed lion for Olivia. Marcus received an infant onesie with Keep Calm My Favorite Auntie Is Here written on the front.

We cleaned up from the gift opening, snapped a few pictures so that our memories would be forever locked in, and then retreated to the basement to hang out and play with the kids. Soon it was dinner time, followed shortly thereafter by bedtime for those who were under the age of four. James and I were enjoying a ukulele concert, complete with singing from Capris and Candace, when Nick and Anna-Marie rejoined us in the dining room.

"You know, it doesn't feel like we just met. Seems like we've known each other for a long time," Anna-Marie said.

I concurred.

CHAPTER 10

Paternity

LITTLE KID SQUEALS AND tiny feet running across the floor above me caused my eyes to open from the previous night's slumber. I was so very thankful my brother and his wife had welcomed us into their home and hearts. It was comfortable there—so natural, so right. Our two families meshed together seamlessly. Our overall outlooks on life, senses of humor, and personalities were well-matched.

My morning prayer included gratitude to God for bringing me to that miraculous day, February 24, 2018. Years of not knowing had come to an end. My birth father held the key to unlock a treasure trove of knowledge, and my ears and brain were eager recipients.

I showered and dressed, then headed upstairs to the kitchen to greet everyone with good morning hugs and kisses. Nick, the master chef, served up a full breakfast spread. James and I took ours to go since we were running a bit late. We were scheduled to meet Daddy at the lab at 11:00 a.m., and we had a two-hour drive ahead of us. I didn't want to be late for one of the most important appointments in my lifetime.

Capris and Candace planned to caravan along with Nick and his family when they traveled to Peoria later that afternoon. We said our temporary goodbyes, then James and I got into my car, Xara, and continued our road trip southward. Naming my vehicles helped me bond with them.

We turned into the near-empty parking lot. A dark-colored SUV sat parked near the lab's main entrance. I caught a glimpse of my birth father's smiling face as we waved to acknowledge each other. I opened my car door just as Daddy stepped out of his. I wasn't nervous at all.

"Sweetheart! Look at you!" Daddy had waited five decades to see his firstborn child in the flesh.

I freed myself from Xara's restraints and lifted my hands to cover my face. I exited my car and stood seven feet away from a man whom I never thought I would meet. The odds were stacked so high—and yet we beat those odds. His outstretched hands pulled me in for a prolonged, deep embrace.

"Ahhh…it's been fifty years…for this moment." His emotion-rich whisper grazed my inner ear and fast tracked on the raceway to my heart. The warmth of his hug melted away any tension that may have been lurking in the depths of my core. Reassurance took up residency and kicked uncertainty out of the door.

"I love you," he whispered in my ear.

Consumed with emotion, tears fell from my eyes. Fifty years for me to hear my daddy's voice in person. Fifty years for me to feel the touch of my father. Fifty years for me to uncover hidden mysteries about my roots.

He was still speaking, but my emotional brain would not let me focus on what Daddy was saying. I savored the moment.

"I love you too, Daddy."

"I missed you."

"I missed you too, Daddy."

"I didn't know," Daddy said in a low voice as he took a step back to get a good look at me. His broad smile showed hints of where the family front tooth gap came from. We laughed and he pulled me in for another rocking side-to-side hug.

"This is your little sister, Devin." She stood a few feet away, waiting patiently to greet me.

"Hello! Hi!" Devin said as she walked toward me with a huge smile and a big hug.

"My man!" Daddy walked toward James to greet him with a handshake and hug.

"How's it going, Pops? It's so good to meet you."

"It's going all right, James." Daddy patted him on the back.

"No crying!" Devin said to me with a lighthearted chuckle.

"I know, I'm crying." I tried to dry my tear-stained cheeks but found my hands to be inadequate tissues. Devin and I looked at each other and went in for another hug.

"How are you? How was your drive?" she asked.

"It was good." I continued to wipe involuntary tears.

"This is a great moment!" James said to Daddy.

"It is!" The jubilation in Daddy's voice was contagious.

The cool Illinois air forced me to put my hands in my pockets as we chatted in the parking lot. Daddy looked at me and said, "You're taller than your mom." We all laughed as Daddy pulled me in for another long hug.

"And you got gray hair." Daddy smiled as he touched my salt-and-pepper locks.

"I do. I have lots of gray hair," I said as I continued to wipe away those pesky tears.

"Well, I don't grow hair anymore." Daddy rubbed his hand in a circular motion across his bald head.

"So you don't know if it's gray or not!" We all laughed at my comment.

We engaged in more small talk before we entered through the doors to the lab. The facility was part of a nationwide franchise that provided full-service diagnostic testing for individuals, organizations, and health care professionals. I found them by doing a Google search for paternity testing in Illinois. We signed in at the front desk and Daddy and I were instructed to fill out the forms that were attached to clipboards, which the receptionist handed to each of us. Besides the normal personal information, the form asked us how we wanted to be notified of the results. Daddy and I specified that we wanted the results mailed via the postal service, as well as emailed. Upon completion of the paperwork, we were led by a middle-aged gentleman down a well-lit hallway and into an examination room.

"Please, have a seat," he said as he motioned toward our two options.

Daddy headed toward the cushioned stool in the center of the room. I opted for the seat near the door we had just entered through. The gentleman walked over to the countertop and explained the process to us.

"May I see your identification?" He stretched his hands toward both of us. Daddy and I each reached into our wallets and gave him our driver's licenses.

"While we do perform legal paternity tests, you have opted for the non-court-admissible test. Your results will be correct in identifying your relationship, but the report cannot be used in a court of law with regards to determining child support responsibilities or other rights or entitlements that go along with a parent/child relationship."

I smiled at Daddy. I had surpassed the child support age limit several times over, so no issues there. Besides, my journey was not about finding monetary riches but about unearthing the priceless jewel of my genealogy.

The gentleman reached up into the cabinet and pulled out a DNA sample collection kit. He put labels on containers and envelopes that would be used to house the buccal swabs.

"Who wants to go first?" He turned around to face us.

"Age before beauty." I waved in Daddy's direction. The gentleman used one swab per cheek to collect cell material from the buccal mucosa, located on the inner wall of Daddy's mouth. He placed the swabs in the containers and envelopes that he had prepared.

I sat in the room and prayed the test results would be conclusive. Daddy's willingness to do the test put my mind at ease. There would be no question or doubt. I suspect there was no doubt in Daddy's mind, but it was comforting to me to know that within a few days the verdict would be in.

The gentleman duplicated the process on me. He informed us that our samples would be sent out via FedEx that afternoon and should arrive at the testing facility by Monday. We should expect to receive the results within five to seven days. We thanked him and exchanged smiles that bore a family resemblance. The gentleman escorted us out of the room and back to the lobby, where James and Devin were chatting.

"All done?" James asked as he looked in our direction and broke from his conversation with Devin.

"Yep! That was easy," I said.

Daddy invited us to his house as we gathered our coats. James offered to take a picture of Daddy and me—our first together. I was so grateful to James for capturing the monumental moments of that day with video and photos.

We parallel parked in front of Daddy's house, which appeared to be deeper than it was wide. One of the pastors from the church next door had lived in it prior to Daddy moving in. The enclosed front porch served as a three-season room, where gentle breezes kissed the screened-in windows on sunny afternoons.

"Let's take your bags upstairs so you can get settled," Daddy said.

James grabbed our suitcase and we followed Daddy up the wooden stairs to the second level. He led us into the guest bedroom. Printed photos taped to the wooden frame of the dresser mirror gave us a glimpse into Daddy's storied life.

"This is Nadine when she was fifteen or sixteen." Her caramel skin tone and curly hair resembled our sister Diana's.

"And that is Anthony when he was in the military. Here's Diana when she came to visit when she was twelve years old.

This is my sister's son. He's now living in your grandma Sylvia's apartment in Manhattan. He inherited it when she passed away."

Next, Daddy pointed to a black-and-white picture of a man wearing army fatigues, standing outside near some brush.

"This picture was taken a year before you were born. I had just come back from delivering messages near the DMZ. I was nineteen. So if your mom was pregnant, then she was three months pregnant at that time.

"And that was my partner. We met in Fort Riley, Kansas, and were stationed in Germany together. There were only fifty black guys in the Criminal Investigation Department at that time. The whole army only had fifty black investigators," Daddy said.

James rubbed his chin and stepped in for a closer look at the black-and-white Polaroid.

"They wanted us to chase dope dealers. We bitched and complained because we were criminal investigators. We wanted to do murder and robbery and that kind of stuff. Finally, they let us do it. Whenever a German got killed and a GI was a suspect, they brought us in to work with the German police, the Kripo—Kriminalpolizei. My partner's mom was German, and his dad was a Black military policeman."

Daddy and his partner had put on their best Starsky and Hutch pose for the camera.

"Let's see what else we got." He pointed to a picture hanging on the wall, an artist's rendition of Jesus standing on the outside of a door. It looked as if He was getting ready to knock or enter. "This painting belonged to your great-grandmother Tanty. After she died, I took it. But you can have this." Daddy handed me a wooden cross with a small symbolic figure of Jesus nailed to it.

"That belonged to your grandmother Sylvia."

How appropriate that my first gift from Daddy was Grandma's emblem of her great faith. My soul was touched as

I was reminded of Jesus's ultimate sacrifice and how He suffered, bled, and died for our sins so that we may have everlasting life in Heaven. My fingers smoothed over the crucifix, and again I thanked my Heavenly Father for the gift of salvation. I was also appreciative for the opportunity to stand next to my biological father and for the gift of my grandmother's cross.

"Thank you! Oh my goodness."

"Great! Now, come downstairs. You can take pictures because she's going to want to see the look on her face." Daddy tilted his head ever so slightly towards James and nodded as a relaxed smile made an appearance beneath his wispy salt-and-pepper mustache. He turned to pick up a metallic silver envelope and held it a few feet from my eyes, hypnotizing me with its iridescence. The envelope contents were quite mysterious. What did Daddy have for me?

"No peeking!" He wiggled his index finger left and right.

"Ok, I won't peek."

James and I exchanged amused glances before following Daddy out of the room and into his office, located in between the guest bedroom and the master bedroom. Pictures of my daughters and me that I had texted him last month were taped on the wall, along with a barrage of photos of other family members, former coworkers, and a *Newsweek* magazine cover graced by Barack Obama.

"I'm into neuroscience in my work…neurobiology. And I usually have my models here. To explain to the kids what's happening inside of them." Daddy picked up a clear plastic bag. "This is a model of a brain. A ten-year-old can take that apart and put it together while we talk."

Daddy walked across the room and pointed to a vintage painted map with hues of blue, orange, yellow, and pale green.

"This is the West Indies…the Caribbean. Puerto Rico, St. Thomas, Anguilla, St. Martin, St. Kitts, Barbuda, Antigua—all the West Indian islands. And, you see, Barbados is the easternmost island in the West Indies. Nothing between Barbados and Africa."

Daddy pointed to another island on the map. "Trinidad. When I left Barbados at sixteen, my father went to Trinidad. He was a bookkeeper and migrated in the late 1950s in search of better wages."

Daddy's attention now turned to other things in the room, which was cluttered with books, toys, papers, office supplies, furniture, and other miscellaneous items. "This is my *DSM*...the bible for psychiatry. My notes, right there. A lot of technical books here. Nick and Devin's brother wrote me that poem up there when he was twelve or so. He thought I was wonderful." I stepped closer to look at the framed literary piece that Daddy cherished from his stepson.

On top of another bookcase, a gold frame held a formal photo of Nick posing with some teammates and a coach from his college football team. A black frame on the far end of the bookcase displayed a picture of Nick, in ready position on the field, wearing his NFL football uniform. A commemorative plate with President Barack Obama was positioned next to Nick's professional football photo, with a framed 8 x 10 portrait of Malcom X rounding out the exhibit of influential black men.

"I sit here and do my work. I'm reading these. This one is in German. These two are psychology texts. And that is my neuroscience." Daddy sifted through three paperback books on a crowded side table.

"My printer, fax machine, heater. Some junk in here." Daddy opened the pull-out drawers of some clear plastic storage bins. They looked just like the ones that were stacked behind his computer monitor. "I know where stuff is, but I don't always know which drawer."

I looked at his organized chaos.

"Here's another bag that I take to my kids. There's all my friends." Daddy pointed to a pile of stuffed animals on the couch. A Smurf, Cat in the Hat, Bullwinkle J. Moose, and the Grinch were all decked out in Christmas holiday attire.

Satisfied that we had covered everything of importance within his office, Daddy led us back down the hardwood stairs and into the great room, where more pictures ornamented the top of a piano.

"All right. The family started with him, my grandfather Nick, also known as Lionel." Daddy pointed to a black-and-white portrait of the professional entertainer. "He was an off-Broadway performer who even did shows in Germany. He had a job too. He was a lithographer. Do you know what that is?"

James shook his head no.

"Back in the day, he ran a machine as big as that room." Daddy pointed to the dining room. "His job was to run the printing press that produced album covers."

"Did he sing in German when they performed in Germany?" James asked.

"Yeah, they sang in German. Nick and Tanty had my mom Sylvia. And Sylvia had four kids. My sister Candy and me are the only ones still living.

"In this picture, my siblings and I are standing with your great-grandma Tanty. We're in Barbados, standing in front of the house we grew up in. It must have been Christmas since the boys are in bow ties. I still remember that suit." The double-breasted two-piece looked like a custom fit for Daddy's slender build. His brothers sported white shirts with dark ties. The short-sleeved dresses Great-grandma Tanty and Aunt Candy wore were in stark contrast to the winter attire featured on our Midwestern holiday greeting card. Made sense for an island with 80°F temperatures in December.

"These are Anthony's kids."

Two framed photo collages, one for each child, exhibited baby pictures of my niece and nephew. Instead of being mounted on a wall, the frames rested on top of an old-style radiator originally installed when the house was built in 1903.

Central heating had taken its functional place and left that relic as part of the centenarian house's charm and décor. I ran my fingers across the radiator, marveling at how I stood in my father's home, with him being only steps away.

The last month had been a blur. I didn't know what I would do if the paternity test came back negative. I didn't want to think about that. Daddy seemed so certain that I was his child. I took that confidence and ran with it.

CHAPTER 11

Grandma's Treasures

DADDY LED THE WAY into the dining room, where we settled down into the chairs. The lace curtains covering the windows allowed the afternoon sun rays to shine in between pockets of rain clouds that started congregating in the distance.

"All right, Ms. Lisa, are you ready for the shock of your life?"

I sat across from Devin, with Daddy sitting at the head of the oval table. I had no idea what to expect.

"When I last talked to you, I didn't have this. It's only been within the last three days. Searching through many, many boxes. I keep everything, sweetheart." Daddy slid the envelope toward me.

I opened the flap to take out the contents. I stared at a sepia photograph. My mouth gaped as my hand moved to cover it. I could not blink. Tears welled up within my eyes. That alert, happy baby staring back at me was *me*. The photographer had managed to capture the tiny spit bubbles that had formed on my lips. My three-month-old self looked a lot like my daughters when they were that age. I had never seen a baby picture of myself.

Me at 100 days old and Candace at 7 months

Daddy wrapped his arms around me and pulled me closer to him for a side hug. He kissed my head as I tried to hold back my tears. The earliest photos I had seen of me were on my Korean passport and United States Naturalization Certificate, both at age two.

"Now you know who you are. You've got your picture." Daddy pointed to Korean writing on the front of the photograph. "You'll have to get that translated. I can't read Korean anymore."

I'd later learn that photo was taken in honor of my "one hundredth day" celebration. Proud parents who could afford elaborate parties gathered with family and friends to pray, feast, and participate in other rituals associated with the milestone. A lot of newborns died due to childhood diseases, lack of medical care, and harsh Korean winters. It was believed that if a baby stayed alive beyond one hundred days, that child would live to celebrate many more birthdays.

Korean age is calculated differently than Western age. Babies exit the womb at age one. Everyone gets another year on New Year's Day. It's all about the number of years a person has experienced during their lifetime. A baby born on the last day of 2018 would turn two on the first day of 2019. In this example, the baby experienced two years, 2018 and 2019, even if those two years were experienced within two days.

I put my baby picture to the side to look at the next picture.

"This is Judy…Chung Suk-ah. That's exactly what she looked like." Daddy's eyes softened as he brushed his finger over my mother's face. I noticed my mother was wearing a ring on her left hand.

"And you think that is her aunt?" I pointed to a woman holding me in the background.

My mother circa 1967

"I think that's ahjussi's wife—her uncle's wife—holding you." Ahjussi is a Korean honorific term used by a woman who is younger than the man she is addressing or referring to. It means middle-aged man or married man in the generation of the speaker's parents.

Cursive handwriting on the back of the photo stated, "Here is another woman embraced my daughter."

Daddy peered at the writing through the bottom half of his glasses. "The translator wrote that." Grammatical errors legitimized his train of thought.

"Can I see that one?" Devin reached for my baby picture.

I slid the photo across the table.

The next picture looked as if it had been taken in a photo studio. It was the same one that he had texted me the first time we spoke. The backdrop displayed an artistic Korean hornbeam bonsai tree with its branches sprawled out against a slate blue and gray sky. My mother wore a traditional long-sleeved, floor-length pink Korean hanbok dress with white tights and black ballerina-style shoes. She completed her look with a sideswept updo for her straight black hair. Umma and Daddy stood side-by-side, their arms locked around each other's waist. His opposite hand rested in his brown suit pants pocket. Daddy's twenty-year-old self bore a strong resemblance to my brother Nick.

"Chung Suk-ah, Nul No Ri, 1967," Daddy read his writing on the back of the picture. "Yeah, she's pregnant. If you'll make copies and send them to me, you can have the originals."

I was in utero. That was the only family picture that existed of the three of us.

James put a box of tissues on the table. I took a few to dry my eyes and tried to keep my runny nose from causing a scene.

"Ah, what do you think of your little self?" Daddy asked. I'm not sure I was cognizant he asked me a question.

"Did you notice that you had a bubble in your mouth? That's a happy baby." Daddy tapped the photo.

"Thank you for finding these." I placed the priceless pictures back on the table and studied each one. Looking back in time captivated me.

"That's crazy!" Devin said as she handed my baby picture back to me.

"She was a cute little baby, right?" said Daddy.

Devin nodded her head.

I took my baby picture in my hand once again.

"I just found that a week ago, going through my papers," Daddy said.

"I don't know how you found it. Like, how did you...?" My voice gave way to the cogs in my mind. They rotated conveyor belts topped with boxes full of reasons why Daddy should not have these pictures. Not only had he kept the pictures—he presented them on demand.

"I don't throw anything away. Do you throw away happiness, man?" Daddy shrugged as he turned to get consensus from James.

"When did you write this?" I pointed to what was written on the back of my baby picture: 1968 Nul No Ri, Korea. Chung Suk-ah is her mother.

"I wrote it sometime after I got it in 1968, but I knew you were born in 1967."

"That makes sense." I flipped the picture back over.

"I told that to Nick. I didn't know if it was July or August, but it was close. Because I knew how pregnant she was."

"That's her," James said after inspecting my baby photo.

Daddy gave an affirmative nod.

I leaned back in my chair and gawked at the historical photographic display laying in front of me. Within the last fifty years, Daddy had resided in multiple countries, married four times, and had six more children. Yet he kept multiple pictures from his time in Korea and offered me the originals.

"Do you want to see the rest?" Daddy had collected several items he wanted to present to me. The first was a magnet with a Barbados street and storefront scene painted by one of his favorite artists. Whenever I visited a city, state, or country for the first time, I was always on the hunt for the perfect magnet to complement my collection. My daughters contributed to my assortment by gifting magnets from places where they'd traveled. Although I had never been to Barbados, that magnet would fit right in with its Caribbean cousins—Puerto Rico, the Dominican Republic, the Cayman Islands, the Bahamas, Jamaica, Turks & Caicos—all family vacation spots.

"Now, you are Barbadian," Daddy's voice boomed.

"I am Barbadian," I repeated as if I was rehearsing lines for an upcoming dramatization.

"Don't say I never gave you any money. Here's a Barbados dollar." Daddy plopped a coin into the palm of my hand. "Don't spend it." Daddy's animated instruction made me laugh. "If you do get to Barbados and want a drink, I'll give you some Barbados money you can spend. That's twenty bucks. It's worth roughly ten US dollars." I graciously accepted his monetary gift.

Daddy handed me a plastic bag that held a delicate gold chain with an opal pendant. "After your grandmother Sylvia died, I removed this from her neck. None of the other kids wanted it. I can't wear it. I don't know if you wear jewelry like that," Daddy said.

"I will keep it. Forever. Thank you." My tone moved to a near whisper as I admired the beauty of the gemstones. I now owned something so personal of my grandmother's.

"Sylvia was good at making sure all the kids got one of these." Daddy reached into his button-up plaid shirt and showed us a gold chain. A gold charm shaped like a map of Barbados dangled from it.

"It has my birthstone in it. I don't wear it because I have sensory processing disorder. Things on my neck bother me. I only put it on for you. See how special you are?" Daddy leaned over and nudged me.

"I'm going to give you your grandmother's." He handed me a sheet of paper with Grandma Sylvia's matching necklace taped to it. Her garnet birthstone was secure in the southwest region of the gold map charm. Grandma's goddaughter gifted her the necklace.

"When was her birthday?" I asked.

"January 23, 1930. And she died November 11, 2010."

I wrote the dates on the piece of paper the necklace was taped to. "And that is Grandma Sylvia's?" I clarified.

"Yes, that's the one she wore. She wore it all the time. She wore both all the time." Daddy pointed to the opal necklace, then to the Barbados necklace, and back again.

I pointed to the opal necklace. "And she was wearing that when she passed away?"

"Right, we were there. You came later, huh?" Daddy looked up at Devin.

"Yeah, me and Nick came to the funeral."

"Diana took a couple of rings and a bracelet when she came." Daddy opened a white sign-in book. "That's the last good picture we have of Grandma Sylvia. You can have one of those if you want. This is the book the church gave us for the visitation. She was always dressed up going somewhere." He smiled as he viewed his beloved mother's photo.

We looked through the funeral sign-in book and Daddy pointed out people who had attended the service and gave me a short bio on each. Some were neighbors, others cousins from Canada or relatives and friends from Barbados. Daddy also explained how the church that Grandma Sylvia attended in Barbados had relocated to Brooklyn.

Daddy stood to find anything else he may have collected.

"I got the best reaction video." Devin looked up from her phone screen. "Your reaction was so good." She had caught my eyebrow crinkle, mouth gape, and those pesky tears tunneling an escape route from my ducts again. Kudos to her for such priceless video footage.

"Here's a bigger envelope for anything else you want to take." Daddy handed me a larger version of the iridescent silver one.

"I'm kinda digging these envelopes, they're fancy." I accepted his offering and collected all of my priceless keepsakes. Those iridescent treasure chests would store my personal heirlooms securely until I could get them home to a safe place.

"All right, here's the fun. I separated out all the pictures I could of family members and people you know or should know." Daddy placed a photo album with a floral cover on the wooden dining room table. He opened it up to a page with vintage pictures of various family members, friends who were family, and high school classmates attached to the aging sheets.

"That's you and your mom standing in front of her house. I couldn't get it out of there without tearing it up. That's what I sent to you."

"That was her house?" I bent over the photo to try to get a better look.

"Yeah, and the door was right behind her. It was a whole compound. There was a kimchi pot buried right there." He pointed to a place in front of where my mother was standing. Kimchi is a mealtime staple in Korea. The fermented cabbage or radish side dish can be quite spicy, and sometimes a bit fishy, but it is always beloved by Koreans young and old. I've heard the nation's emigrants often suffer withdrawal when they move to a country that does not offer them the opportunity to eat it with every meal.

The opposite page in the photo album had pictures of Daddy's siblings. He explained to us the close relationship his immediate family had shared with another family growing up and pointed out his bonus sisters and brother. He told us stories of how, at an early age, he had followed those sisters to their all-girls school because he didn't want to be left at home. It didn't matter to him that he would be the only boy there.

"The teacher said I could come if I knew my ABCs. I could recite them when I was three and a half, so I was able to go to school with them."

Daddy pointed out more pictures of Grandma Sylvia and Great-grandma Tanty, and even a picture of Great-grandpa Nick—"Lionel, the grandfather that brought us here."

It was interesting to me that everyone had more than one name. Daddy had mentioned Great-grandpa Nick a few times but why did he also go by Lionel? And Great-grandma Tanty's name was Fredricka, but she was known to her friends as Rita. Daddy's sister Gloria was known as Candy. And Daddy told me about his friend's sister, whose name was Patsy, who now called herself Toni. Why so many names? Daddy didn't have an answer.

"I just got a text from the girls. They're pulling up." Devin walked with me to the front door.

"Are they here?" Daddy looked through the glass.

"It's Auntie Devin!" one of the girls said as they walked up the stairs towards the porch. My baby sister opened the door and I introduced her to her nieces.

"How's it going?" The pair hugged.

"Hi, good!" Capris reciprocated her aunt's embrace, then turned toward her grandfather. She greeted him with a huge smile, and he responded with a kiss to her cheek as they came together for a hug.

"Welcome, sweetheart!" Daddy took a step back to get a better look at his granddaughter as Devin and Candace greeted each other with smiles and hugs.

"Chung Suk-ah," Daddy gave Candace a kiss on the cheek before they hugged. The first time he had seen a picture of his granddaughter, he declared she had her grandmother's eyes.

"Come on in, let me get your coat." Daddy helped to get the girls situated before moving into the living room.

I let Capris and Candace have a front-row seat so they could learn the history of their ancestors.

Before long there was a knock at the door. My brother Anthony walked in and greeted me with a big hug.

"You look so much younger than me!" he said. The gray hair sprinkled throughout his beard, along with a receding hairline, gave his observation some merit.

He introduced me to his children. My niece and nephew both stood nearly as tall as me. Not a surprise—most kids surpass me in height by the age of thirteen.

"Got to get a selfie." Anthony pulled out his phone and motioned for me to stand beside him. He hugged me again after our impromptu photo shoot.

"Now," he said, "you have to tell me everything."

CHAPTER 12

Party of 21

LIGHT DROPLETS OF RAIN sprinkled the windshield as James parked in the rear lot. Excitement from meeting my father and two more siblings hours earlier had curbed my appetite, but we had early dinner reservations for 4:00 p.m. Nadine and Rob stood near the hostess stand inside Olive Garden. We weaved through the crowded waiting area to greet my sister and brother.

"Well, hello there!" I said. I recognized them from the pictures Diana had sent.

Rob turned and smiled at me. He outstretched his six-foot wingspan and I nestled in for a warm hug.

"Hello, Lisa, how are you?" said Rob.

"I'm good, it's good to see you!" I stepped back to get a good look at my younger brother. He introduced me to his wife before I turned to greet my sister.

"Hi, Nadine!" She stood nearby. Her beautiful smile and deep dimples were striking.

"Hello, how are you?" she said as she hugged me, with her one-year-old daughter perched on her opposite side.

"Hello, sweetie, how are you?" My niece grasped my finger as I raised my hand to touch hers.

I bent down to greet my two-year-old nephew. He flashed me a cute smile and a wave.

Nadine introduced us to her husband before turning to greet mine.

"And you must be James," Nadine said as she walked toward him. "I don't know if you're a hugger or a handshaker."

"Oh, I'm a hugger," he said as they embraced.

We waited ten minutes before the hostess called out "Nadine, party of twenty-one."

I enjoyed watching everyone interact. Little did I know the family gathering that night was full of firsts. Nick and Nadine had never met each other's children. Nadine's husband had never met Nick or Anna-Marie. Daddy had never met Rob's wife, even though she and my brother had been married for six years and had dated for a number of years before that. Another notable first was that Rob had never met Anna-Marie or her and Nick's kids. That dinner wasn't just about me connecting with my family. It was more about my family reconnecting with each other.

"I chose this restaurant because they have good vegan options and menu items for the kids," Nadine said.

"I didn't know you were vegan," I said.

"We all are," said Nadine's husband.

"Daddy told me that Aunt Candy used to be vegan, but she isn't anymore. Nadine, do you like to cook?"

"Yes, which is a good thing," she responded. "We don't have a lot of options at many restaurants."

The servers were very attentive to our large group. The manager brought us a surprise with our dessert. He placed on the table a white serving plate with "Family Love" written in strawberry red syrup. Five asterisks were positioned around the phrase, written in the same red edible gel. Three decorative dollops of whipped cream adorned the right-hand side of the plate, each one topped with an Andes chocolate mint. That was such a thoughtful gesture.

It was indeed a great night of family love. My biological siblings and their immediate families were all present. Daddy video called Diana so she could join in from Germany. There were plenty of handshakes, hugs, and smiles that erupted into laughter. We commemorated the gathering with group photos, and I gave Nadine and Rob the gifts I had brought for them from Nebraska before we parted ways for the evening.

What a day it had been. It didn't feel like we had just met. The instant bond not only happened for me but for my husband and daughters as well. Now they would also get to form their own relationships with in-laws, grandparents, aunts, uncles, and cousins.

Siblings: Nick, Devin, Lisa, Anthony, Diana, Rob, and Nadine

After leaving the restaurant, James drove to Daddy's house. Inside, Daddy moved in sync with the music. Candace joined her grandfather on the living room dance floor. They both danced and sang, each giving the other a bow and thanking one another for the dance once the song finished.

"I need to charge my phone," said Capris.

"You can use my charger." I handed her my power bank.

"Thanks, I have about fourteen percent. Wait…what just happened?" Capris stared at her black phone screen, pushing the power button multiple times.

"What's wrong, it won't come on?" The screen was black.

"It still had a little bit of juice left, but after I plugged it into the charger it just died."

I reached for her phone. "Here, let me take a look at it." I tried all my tricks of the trade but was unsuccessful at resuscitating her device.

"I just lost all of the photos and videos from this weekend." She had been the self-designated photographer/videographer for that trip, and her devastation was heartbreaking.

"Well, maybe we can get them from a backup. Did your phone back up to iCloud last night?"

"No, because I wasn't connected to Wi-Fi at Nick's." She found it difficult to mask the sadness in her tone.

"And now how am I supposed to navigate back home tomorrow? I was using it as my GPS. And I have volleyball practice at 6:00 p.m. tomorrow, and I can't text anyone, and they can't get ahold of me, either." Her mounting frustration was evident upon her brow.

"Now, that might be a problem. Let's unplug it from the charger and plug it into an outlet to see if it will power on once it's been connected for a while. It's ok, honey, other people were taking pictures, so we'll have some, and you took some with your GoPro, right?"

"Yes, but I also took some with my phone, and now they're gone. What am I supposed to do?" Capris's shoulders drooped as she stared at her lifeless device. She looked as if she was trying to mentally will it back to life.

Fortunately, Capris's phone was still under warranty, so we made plans to take it into an Apple Store the next morning.

I was thankful that other people had been taking pictures, and I was prayerful that her phone issues would get resolved before her road trip home.

With all the activities of the last couple of days, I found it easy to slip into a deep slumber as soon as my head hit the pillow. It was all still very surreal, but I soaked in each moment, praying that I would not wake up and realize that it was all a dream. Well, it was a dream—come true.

CAPRIS AND I ARRIVED at the open-air shopping center at 10:30 a.m. A line had already formed outside of the Apple Store's front doors. Did the start of each retail day begin like that? At 10:45, several store employees came out and interviewed everyone, uncovering the nature of their visit.

We were instructed to go to the Genius Bar. A young man in his early thirties offered assistance and listened as Capris described the problem she'd experienced. Capris stared blankly ahead as he troubleshot her device. He took her phone and disappeared into the back. When he returned, he informed us it would be at least an hour before her phone would be fixed—not what Capris wanted to hear, since she had a four hour drive home, and she wanted to say goodbye to everyone before she returned to Des Moines.

"Walking around the mall will kill some time." Even though retail therapy would not help her mood, Capris agreed, and we browsed in some of the shops until the Apple Geniuses finished working their magic on her phone.

"It's too late for me to make it to practice now."

"I'm sorry, honey. But on the bright side, your phone is fixed. Nick said he picked up some food for us, so let's go by his mom's house to eat."

Nick's mom lived in a two-story duplex in an established neighborhood with mature trees and wide four-lane streets. The winter air was cool, but not uncomfortably cold. Springtime was right around the corner. We ventured up the concrete steps onto the wooden porch and rang the doorbell.

"Hey there, come on in!" Anna-Marie opened the door and greeted both of us with a hug.

"Hello, everyone," I said as I entered the living room where my nieces and nephews were playing with their Auntie Devin.

"Hey, y'all," Nick called out from the kitchen. James arrived just in time for us to start devouring the gyros my brother had bought from one of his favorite places in the city.

"What time are you guys heading out?" Nick asked.

"James and I aren't leaving until tomorrow morning." I took another bite of a ketchup-dipped french fry and washed it down with water. "We're going to stop by Daddy's so Capris can say goodbye before she leaves this afternoon."

We finished our meal and played with the kids until nap time. We said our goodbyes to everyone before heading down the alley.

"Hey there," Daddy greeted us. "Capris, did you get your phone fixed?"

"Yep. It took longer than expected, but it's fixed."

"She missed her volleyball practice, but now at least she will have navigation on her trip home," I said.

"That's good." Daddy walked into the living room and sat in his favorite rocking chair.

"I just stopped by to say goodbye. I'm getting on the road now. I don't want it to be too late when I get back home."

"As long as you come back. You're always welcome. Don't stay away too long," Grandpa commanded.

"I'll definitely be back," Capris said as she laughed. She gave hugs all the way around, then the rest of us huddled around the front door and watched as she descended the steps.

Once her car was out of sight, I turned and said, "Daddy, you should open your present."

"Oh yes, that's right, you handed it to me yesterday. Let's see, it's right here." Daddy put the wrapped package on his lap after sitting in his rocker. I wanted Daddy's gift to be unique and personal. I had used my computer to create a design for a canvas. The Barbadian flag, in the shape of the island, appeared on the left, and the South Korean flag, in the shape of the Republic of Korea, appeared on the right. Situated between the two mapped landmasses was this message: "When Barbados and South Korea Come Together ♥ A Little Happiness Is Born." The design was set against a pale cyan background and mounted to a black wooden frame.

"Baby girl, a lot of happiness is born!" Daddy said as he took a good look at his gift.

"I guess Nick's not the only artistic one in the family. I'll hang in the spare bedroom." Daddy placed the original artwork on the table until he was ready to take it upstairs.

"Now lemme see what your Aunt Candy is up to." Daddy dialed his sister's cell phone number and put her on speakerphone as she answered.

"Hello?" My aunt greeted her brother in her New York accent.

"Hey, Candy, I want introduce you to your niece."

"Lisa?"

"Hi, Aunt Candy."

"Hi, Lisa, how are you doing?"

"I'm good, it's nice to meet you. My husband, James, is here too."

"Hello there," James said.

"Hello, how are you all doing over there?"

"We're good. Hey, Candy, do you have FaceTime? So we can video chat?" Daddy asked.

"FaceTime? Well, I don't know…where is that?"

"It's on your phone. Look on your phone," Daddy said.

"No, I don't see it."

"Does she have an iPhone?" I asked. "Because if not, then she won't have FaceTime. If she has WhatsApp, we can video chat with that."

"Gloria, you got that?" Daddy asked.

"Got what?" Aunt Candy asked.

"WhatsApp," Daddy said.

"Uh, let's see. I think so, but I'm not sure where to find it."

"That's ok. If you find it later, we can video chat some other time," I said.

"Oh ok. Now, Lisa, when are you going to come to upstate New York to visit me? It's beautiful up here and you need to come sooner than later."

I looked at Daddy and smiled. "Maybe I'll have to plan a trip within the next few months."

"Oh, that would be wonderful. We have a lot of nice walking trails and there is so much to do and see."

"What airport do I fly into?"

"You fly into Stewart."

"Or you might consider flying into JFK or Newark and taking the train," Daddy said.

"No, that's too far. The Amtrak to Poughkeepsie will get her close to me."

"I can figure it out. I've got some time," I said.

"Let me know when you plan to come."

"All right, Candy, see if you have video chat and we'll talk later," Daddy said.

The 6:00 p.m. hour was upon us. I had told Anthony that we would spend time together that evening after he got off work, since James and I would be heading home the next day.

Anthony's Japanese mother and our father met in Okinawa after Daddy left South Korea. They married before Daddy's orders to go to Germany were issued. Apparently, by 1969, the army had changed its stance on soldiers marrying their Asian girlfriends. Anthony and his mother accompanied Daddy to Germany, where they had a second child. Unfortunately, Anthony's infant sibling passed away from crib death in the early 1970s, at the age of one.

My brother's mother left our father and Germany and took Anthony back to Okinawa with her when he was three years old. His early life was a bit rough. His mother enrolled him in a Catholic school in Okinawa where they taught English, but he had a challenging time excelling there. The end result was that he couldn't read Japanese or English very well.

When Anthony turned twelve, his mother sent him to Germany to live with our father. By that time, Daddy had married for the second time.

"When my mother told me I was going to go live with Daddy, I was super excited," Anthony told me. "I thought it was going to be great, just me and Dad. Boy, was I surprised to find out that he was married and I had a little sister, Nadine. No one mentioned any of that to me."

When Daddy and I discussed it later, he said, "My wife, at the time, was thrown into an unexpected situation. Anthony's mom dropped him off to me in Germany on Mother's Day. I was in the military and gone for days at a time on assignment. My wife had no choice but to take care of him. And from an academic perspective, Anthony was far behind other kids his age. When I looked at the big picture, he didn't have a chance at being successful if we stayed in Germany. The school system there would have forced him to make a career path decision before he was mentally equipped to do so. I couldn't do that to him. I wanted to give him the best chance at life."

Daddy's wife had family in Illinois, which would make her transition back to the US a bit easier. But for reasons unbeknownst to me, their marriage struggled and ended in divorce after Rob was born.

Anthony said he physically fought his way through many situations during his youth, earning the reputation for being a 5'5" badass.

I don't condone fighting, but physical altercations amongst fellow students in the 1970s was commonplace. Back then, school fights didn't include the use of guns or knives. We used our fists—or in my case, my mouth—as weapons. Meeting on the playground after school meant combatting classmates would find themselves in the principal's office the next day, or

in after school detention. I was no stranger to the latter. The
detention monitor commanded me to write "I will not fight
after school" on the chalk board. Writing that phrase one
hundred times normally took up the whole hour. Good thing
there was a late school bus I could catch to get me home.

My parents taught me to never instigate fights, but I could
stand up for myself if someone started one with me. When you
are small in stature, bigger kids think they have the advantage.
Like my brother, I also had to defend my way through being
bullied. On one occasion, my battle got me suspended from
riding the school bus. That altercation left a lasting impression
on the classmate that had initiated it. Thirty years after that
incident, he told me the bite mark I had left on his arm served
as a visual reminder for years. We were able to laugh about it
as adults.

I LAY IN BED in my father's house, staring at the picture-
adorned walls. My mind went back to dinner the night before,
the historic gathering of Daddy, my siblings, and our
immediate families. My prayer that night was one of
immeasurable gratitude for the love that surrounded that table.

James and I slept in the next morning but skipped
breakfast. We wanted to make it back to Omaha before dark.

Daddy handed me a 4 x 6 envelope before I left, which I
opened when I got home. My first and last name were written
on the front in very neat penmanship. I opened it to reveal
hues of blue, green, gold, and splashes of burgundy fashioned
into a beautiful crest on the inside of the unsealed flap. I
removed and unfolded the stationery, which had the same
crest-like image in the upper left-hand corner, set to a beige
background. The letter was penned in cursive handwriting
which matched the envelope.

2-24-2018

Dear Lisa,

Today was one of the happiest days of my long life.
It was made so that I could complete a long wait to
find out what happened to you. All the years I
wondered and tried to explain to Sylvia why I could
not find her grandbaby. Now, at fifty, you have
found us. All is well that ends well. I had lost hope
of finding you, but your grandmother never gave
up. She would be delirious over the news that you
have taken your rightful place as big sister among
us. Welcome. We have missed you. But now you
are here, never to leave, until death parts us.

Love, Daddy

His note filled me with emotion because I understood that
many adoptees wouldn't receive the same welcome from their
birth parents and biological families. It's difficult to know the
circumstances our parents found themselves in when we were
conceived and born. It's even harder to comprehend the
aftermath and trauma which ensued.

My heart is pained whenever I read stories of adoptees who
find relatives that do not want to meet them. Rejection piled
on top of abandonment is a harsh reality in the adoptee
community. Sometimes biological siblings are angry with their
birth parents for deep dark family secrets that come to light at
unexpected times. Even so, I encourage anyone to avoid
extending that rage to estranged brothers and sisters who are
just as much victims of those less than optimal situations. Get
to know them before judging their character.

Was I mentally prepared for the possibility my maternal
tribe may refute my existence, or rebuff my desire to establish
a relationship? I didn't want to give those negative thoughts
any energy or live my life based on what-ifs.

CHAPTER 13

Further Revelations

I STARTED TUESDAY MORNING on a natural high from the weekend's events. I got out of bed and tried to go through my morning ritual as if nothing was new in my life. I drove the same route to work and greeted my coworkers as if normalcy was still a thing of the present. However, my life had been forever changed. My blood relatives lived within a day's driving distance of my home. I had learned about my roots and my ancestors and had so many questions answered.

I reflected on the paternity test that Daddy and I had taken on Saturday and was anxious to learn the results. I checked my email on the off chance that they had already sent the info. My eyes opened wider as I read the invitation sent from the lab to view a shared file. I clicked on the link within the message and analyzed the results. Probability (w = 50%) = 99.9999%. Daddy and I had matched on every single allele, indicating that he was my biological father. All twenty-two chromosomes reflected proof positive that modern-day miracles do exist.

THE OTHER TWO CONSUMER DNA test results were emailed to me a week after I received my mind-blowing Ancestry test outcome in January 2018.

I opened the MyHeritage email first. I was interested to see how close their ethnicity estimate was to Ancestry's.

Asia 53%	
East Asia	
Mongolian	20
Japanese	17
Chinese/Vietnamese	15
Central Asia	1
Africa 43%	
West African	
Nigerian	29
Sierra Leonean	8
West African	4
Central African	1
North African	1
Europe 4%	

I found it intriguing that my ethnicity estimate did not include Korea, but included a large percentage of Mongolian DNA. The difference might be due to Ancestry reporting my ethnicity from a more recent generation, like within the last one hundred years. MyHeritage could have reported it beginning centuries earlier.

Out of 345 DNA matches, my closest relationship was a third cousin, and the most shared DNA segments with anyone was two.

MyHeritage's chromosome browser graphically displayed shared segments. However, that was one of the site's few free tools. Many of the other tools required a paid subscription to access information such as public records and research data.

I pulled up the 23andMe results next. I was curious to see how closely they matched the other two DNA tests.

East Asian/Native American 51.6%	
South Korean	23.7
Manchurian/Mongolian	7.1
Siberian	2.5
Chinese	1.0
Filipino/Austronesian	0.5
Indonesian/Thai/Khmer/Myanmar	0.3
Broadly Chinese/SE Asian	3.8
Broadly Northern Asian/Native American	2.2
Broadly Japanese/Korean	0.6
Broadly East Asian/Native American	9.9
Sub-Saharan African 41.3%	
Ghanaian/Liberian/Sierra Leonean	8.6
Nigerian	6.3
Senegambian/Guinean	5.8
Southern East African	1.0
African Hunter-Gatherer	0.4
Congolese	0.2
Sudanese	0.2
Broadly West African	13.3
Broadly Congolese & Southern E. African	0.2
Broadly Northern E. African	0.1
Broadly Sub-Saharan African	5.2
European 5.7%	
French/German	0.7
Broadly NW European	1.7
Broadly Southern European	1.0
Broadly European	2.3
Unassigned 1.4%	

Out of the 1103 DNA matches that 23andMe identified for me, only two were in the second cousin to third cousin range, and both matched in the Asian region:

NaS
Second Cousin
3.07% DNA shared
11 segments

LP
Second to Third Cousin
1.24% DNA shared
6 segments

Inquiries to both matches via the site's messaging platform went unanswered. Perhaps NaS didn't speak English since he was 100% Korean. I asked an acquaintance to help me compose a message to him in Hangul. Still no response.

LP did respond via social media. She was also an adoptee and knew no biological family, and she had no interest in meeting me.

23andMe gave an in-depth explanation of haplogroups, which detailed maternal lineage and early ancestor migration paths. Mitochondrial DNA is only inherited from our mother's side. That maternal lineage can be traced back thousands of years due to its slow mutative nature. Every member of a specific haplogroup shares a common ancestor. Groups are assigned a letter designation that corresponds to a major branch of the lineage tree, followed by successive numbers and letters that give exact tree branch relationships.

In 23andMe's database, 1 in 2400 people share my maternal haplogroup of M7c1. NaS's haplogroup is M7c1a. This may mean that he and I have a common recent ancestor, like a great-grandmother, for example. The M haplogroup is a branch off of L3, which is the main group to which present-day humans who have origins outside of Africa belong. A significant percentage of the genetic population in Asia are members of the M haplogroup.

23andMe had detailed online articles for each region it indicated I was from, covering topics such as traditions, festivals, and cuisine.

The health predisposition, wellness, carrier status, and traits reports were informative. I didn't understand how my DNA indicated that my earlobes were detached, and my ring finger was longer than my index finger. It was interesting to note that my genetics indicated I was predisposed to developing type 2 diabetes. Daddy had told me the disease ran in my family.

MY INTENSE DESIRE TO reconnect with my birth mother grew a new sense of urgency. I initiated another birth family search through Holt International by filling out their online request form. Unlike in 2015, this time they were able to confirm they had facilitated my adoption, and they emailed me documents that were excluded from the packet that had been given to my parents. Those papers helped uncover clues and answered questions about my life prior to the time I spent at the orphanage.

I double-clicked on one of the attachments to open it. The first page of the document had a photo of my adoptive family that I'd never seen before. The picture was taken in the late 1960s, when the family lived in Okinawa. Judging from the binoculars around my dad's neck, they must have been sightseeing on a high elevation overlooking the Pacific Ocean. I could smell the tobacco smoke from Dad's pipe in his mouth—a scent that took me back to my childhood.

Miles, Clayton, Dad, and Mom circa 1966

Halfway down the page, "Child Name: Lee Augustine" was written above a picture of me taken when I was two years old. Facing the camera with an expressionless face, my hands were cupped together, with my toddler body dressed in a short dress and matching jacket.

A Social History Supplement Report specified my birth mother's name was Lee, Ok Soon, with July 15, 1945, listed as her birthdate. I'm not sure why this information was omitted from the paperwork my parents had. Those documents said my mother and father were unknown, but obviously the adoption agency had pertinent information they withheld in my file.

According to the report, when she relinquished me, she appeared healthy yet somewhat aggressive. She was Korean with no education and was reluctant to give her full address. Her mother died when my mom was three years old. Her father was kidnapped to the north during the Korean War. She had two older siblings, a brother and sister, who were both married. Six years prior, she ran away from home and didn't let her siblings know her whereabouts.

My mother had given the orphanage information on my birth father. She told them he was a military soldier and his family lived in New York. The form listed his name and his

Christian religious affiliation and described him as being healthy, lively, and taciturn. The latter was such an odd English word to have on a Korean document. Perhaps its meaning had been lost in translation.

It detailed my parents' relationship, from my mother's point of view. I was fortunate to have heard the story from my father, but it was interesting to hear it from my mom, albeit through typewritten words on a report a half-century old.

She stated they met each other at her home in Paju, where they lived for one year. Mom acknowledged she was six months pregnant when Daddy received orders to leave Korea. She said he sent her one hundred dollars once, and Grandma Sylvia wrote her two or three times. After she received news that he was going to Vietnam, she never heard from him again.

Did Grandma Sylvia tell her that Daddy was going to Vietnam? I didn't recall him mentioning anything like that.

The report continued to recount how my parents lived together in peace and harmony and how Daddy could write in Korean, which facilitated a good understanding between them. Alas, my mother said she believed in vain that he would come back to her.

The document also stated I lived with an uncle for a year before my mother brought me to the orphanage. Caregivers noted that I seemed to have an extreme longing for my father, and whenever I was told I would be taken to him, I would stop fretting and get ready to go. Perhaps I thought my uncle was my father?

My mother stated she wanted to make sure I would be well cared for and adopted into a family who could provide me with a good emotional environment.

Also included in the packet was a letter signed "Augustine's Pomo." I asked the adoption agency to explain what that was and they informed me that pomo, also spelled bomo (보모), was a general name for a foster mother, caretaker, babysitter, or staff worker. Several children in the same age range lived in each room at the orphanage, and the women who cared for the children assigned to a room were called pomos. According to the adoption agency, it appeared my family had sent me something before I was able to go to the United States, and the pomo thanked them for it and sent my parents an update on me. It was rare for this type of letter to be included in an adoption file, since everything was typewritten on a typewriter and not always in duplicate.

A month after receiving my child materials from the United States-based adoption agency, I received my file from Holt Korea. Their records did not contain complete identifying information for my birth mother, and she had not tried to contact them since my intake.

Current Korean regulations stipulate that a search can only be conducted when the adoption agency can provide the birth parent's complete name and identification number to Korea Adoption Services (KAS). However, Holt Korea offered to submit my search based on the limited information they possessed, with the understanding that it may not be effective. They wanted me to be prepared for a long time frame and the possibility of a negative outcome.

There was no fee for the assisted search, but due to the high volume of travelers to Korea during the summer, service response times could be slower than expected.

In July 2018, I received notice from Holt International that the search for my mother had been unsuccessful, but that my letter and photos would be kept in my file. They closed my case but would reopen it if new information surfaced.

If I waited a year or two, I could request the agency reopen the case to see if my mother updated her information with the government. In my mind, going that route would be a waste of time. If she hadn't legally registered within the last fifty years, why would she ever? All Korean citizens are required by law to register with the government, but not everyone complies. People can move, without updating their address, and still be able to receive mail and work. Another brick wall. The more challenging it became, the more motivated I was to locate her. Even if I found out that she had died, at least I would go to my grave knowing that I had done everything within my means to reach out.

The adoption agency provided options for individual search recommendations if I wanted to continue on my own. Global Overseas Adoptees' Link (G.O.A.'L) was one of the reputable organizations that Holt referred. They responded with two relevant ways to search for my birth family. The first, an active search, would require me to travel to Korea. They would provide volunteers to accompany me and assist with translation and distributing flyers with my story and picture. In my case, G.O.A.'L thought it might be interesting for me to visit the small rural village where my mom once lived. Korean natives tended to be much more helpful with information when speaking face-to-face.

The second option was to request a police search. My case would be turned over to the Korean authorities with hopes they would be willing to assist and follow up on any leads that may come from KAS or G.O.A.'L. I was surprised to learn that this was even an option. Either way, it was going to take a long time to receive an answer (positive or negative).

Plans to visit Korea were not in my immediate future, but I was curious about the First Trip Home program that G.O.A.'L offered. Its main focus was birth family search, with cultural immersion and sightseeing woven in. It was open to adoptees worldwide, who hadn't been back to Korea since their adoption. I asked when the application would be available for the 2019 summer trip and if family members were allowed to accompany participants. They informed me the application and interview process would begin in February or March 2019 and the trip was for adoptees only. It could be difficult for non-adoptees to understand what we are really looking for or what we are expecting from such a unique experience.

Traveling halfway around the world by myself on such a mission seemed a bit daunting at first. I wouldn't be able to lean on my husband for emotional support or have a friend with me to help analyze my journey, but after giving it much thought, I understood their stance. They didn't want participants to worry if their travel partner was ok, or if their kids were bored. All energy needed to be focused on finding family and reconnecting with our Korean roots.

CHAPTER 14

Two Weddings

NADINE TEXTED ME SOME welcome news. She was getting married on a weekend when I had plans to be in town. A few weeks prior, Devin and I had already decided to meet in Peoria during her spring break. I burst at the seams with joy and excitement when Nadine invited both Devin and me to join in the festivities. I WAS GOING TO ATTEND MY SISTER'S WEDDING. Unreal. Two months ago, I hadn't even known I had a sister.

Weddings are very personal life events. Brides and grooms surround themselves with people who are important to them and whom they enjoy being around.

Even though we were biological relatives, we had just met, and I would have understood if Nadine preferred that I not come. Other than Nadine's fiancé, their children, and Rob, the people whom Nadine was the closest to in her life had never met Devin or me.

Fri, Mar 23, 5:33 PM

> I am sooooo excited and I can't begin to describe the joy in my heart!!! Thank you for allowing me to share in your special day. I think I've mentioned before that I always wanted a sister growing up. And now, to be able to be there for my sister on her wedding day...I am overjoyed 🌼

Unfortunately, James was unable to accompany me on that trip, so Xara and I had quality windshield time. I planned to stay with Daddy on Wednesday, attend Nadine's wedding on Thursday, and then Devin and I would meet Capris and Candace at Nick's on Friday.

I HAD NO IDEA who else was attending the wedding. Was Daddy invited? Time would tell.

"Are you up?" Daddy peeked his head through the half-open doorway.

"Good morning, Daddy. How are you?"

"I'm doing all right. Breakfast is ready."

"I'll be right down."

I finished applying my makeup and put my stuff away before descending the wooden steps to the main floor.

I placed a few pieces of cantaloupe on my plate, along with a pastry, and sat with Daddy at the dining room table.

"What are your plans for today?" Daddy asked.

"Devin and I are going to hang out. I told her I would pick her up. I'll be back this afternoon."

I finished my breakfast and gave him a hug before walking out the door. I drove around the corner and waited for Devin to come to the car.

"Does Daddy know about the wedding?" I asked as she fastened her seat belt.

"I'm not sure. I have no idea who is going to be there," she said.

"I know, me neither. I didn't want to ask Daddy about it just in case he didn't know. I didn't want it to be awkward."

"I know, right?" Devin said. It warmed my heart to see her wearing the Love You More bracelet I had given her when we met for the first time in February.

The drive downtown was less than ten minutes. We found a parking spot and walked two blocks to the courthouse entrance. The weather was decent enough that we didn't have to be bundled up. We walked halfway around the building to find an open entrance due to building renovations.

Twenty people had congregated in the hallway leading to the courtrooms. I caught a glimpse of Rob as we stepped out of the elevator.

"Hey, I didn't know you were going to be here!" My brother's outstretched arms greeted us.

"When Nadine told me the date, I let her know Devin and I were both planning on already being in town," I said.

"It's good to see you." Rob turned to his childhood neighbor, whom he had been speaking to before we walked up. "These are my sisters, Lisa and Devin." Small talk ensued for several minutes until Nadine exited the elevator, carrying her daughter on her hip. Underneath her sheer white tutu, my niece had lost a shoe in transit. Nadine greeted her guests as she walked by them down the hallway. I heard some of them ask where her future husband and son were.

"They'll be right up. He's parking."

We helped Nadine with her coat so that she could get her daughter situated. My sister looked stunning. Her curled pixie cut framed her face. Deep dimples and her inherited London Gap accompanied her smile. Her half-sleeved white satin midi dress, with its deep V-neck and fitted bodice, was tailored at the waist before it flared out into a fuller skirt. The spring mix of blue hydrangeas and peach roses with wisps of baby's breath accents made one of the prettiest bouquets I'd ever seen. Rose gold heels and minimalist jewelry made up the finishing touches of Nadine's wedding ensemble.

Her soon-to-be husband appeared with their son. The toddler looked like a tiny model from a wedding magazine spread. He tugged on his blue patterned bow tie, but my gaze was drawn to his two-year-old golden-brown curls, pulled into a man bun on top of his head.

I dug into my purse and pulled out the garter belt I had worn on my own wedding day. I asked Nadine if she would like to wear it, and she graciously accepted. She placed the purple and white garter belt high up on her thigh before scurrying off, trying to figure out if we were in the right place or if the courtroom number had changed. She walked by a couple of times with the garter belt circling her ankle. Each time, she paused long enough to reposition it back to her upper thigh.

"The ceremony is going to take place in the judge's chambers," Nadine announced as she whisked by, my stretched-out garter belt at her ankle again. I didn't want to test her trip avoidance maneuvers, so I caught up to her and offered to rid her of the borrowed and baggy garter.

"It's probably best that I take it off, it won't stay up. But thank you, it was a nice thought."

"Yeah, no worries," I said as I shoved the twenty-six-year-old garter into my purse. Funny, that had worked out differently in my mind.

The wedding guests filed into the judge's chambers, where it was standing room only. The happy couple stood, facing each other with the American flag as their backdrop.

Gratefulness filled my heart as I witnessed my sister exchange sacred vows with her husband.

A downtown restaurant was the after-ceremony spot.

"The entrance is in that back alley." Devin pointed toward a small roadway between multiple buildings.

"Seriously?" How unusual for the main entrance of a popular eatery to be off the beaten path.

We followed some wedding guests on foot down the alleyway. Fellow patrons informed us that there was a password to get in. The price of not knowing was having to do some sort of Simon Says test to prove that you were not a spy and were worthy of entry.

Devin and I entered. We didn't know the password. The restaurant host commanded us to quack like ducks and instructed us to search for some imaginary thing that could be anywhere in the 10 x 12 room in which we were trapped. When Control was satisfied that we were not double agents, they granted us access to the restaurant upstairs. Restaurant diners had the pleasure of viewing the antics on closed-circuit TV screens sprinkled throughout the dining area.

Devin and I congratulated the bride and groom and chatted with my sister's childhood neighbors, while sitting at the bar. It was a fun experience for me to get to know people who knew my family longer than I did.

When Devin and I drove back to Daddy's house, he greeted us at the door.

"Where'd you two go?"

"Downtown," Devin replied.

I looked at her and smiled.

"What did you do downtown?"

"We went to see some people."

I turned my back to them and suppressed the little girl giggles that tried to escape. I set my coat down, then removed my shoes—slowly.

"What people?"

"We saw some people at the courthouse."

Tears of laughter formed in my eyes, but I couldn't let the sound escape. I was still removing my shoes.

"What were they doing at the courthouse?"

Devin paused for a split second before saying, "Nadine got married."

I turned around to look at Daddy's reaction.

"Oh ok. Good for her." He shrugged and leaned against the stairway banister.

"It was nice," Devin said. "Well, my mom is waiting for me to go to the store. I'm going to head out."

"We'll see you later." Daddy and Devin finished their goodbye with a hug and love yous. Devin turned and gave me a hug.

"Love you. See you tomorrow. Tell your mom hi for me," I said with a big smile.

I followed Daddy into the dining room and texted Devin as we sat down at the table.

Thu, Apr 5, 2:52 PM

Sorry I was of no help when Daddy was asking you where we went. I kept my back turned because I was DYING LAUGHING 💀 💀 💀 💀

Hahahaha not a problem at all! I knew he wouldn't really care!! 😂 😂 😂

She knew him better than I did. I didn't have a good grasp on how my family members interacted with each other and I was still trying to figure everyone out. I didn't want to disrupt the family dynamic but I sensed it could be changing with positive momentum.

DIANA AND I COMMUNICATED for over a year via video chats and messaging. Our first in-person meeting happened at the Frankfurt Airport. Thank goodness my international cell phone plan worked. We spotted one another from opposite ends of the terminal. I ran past travelers who had no idea how long it had taken for me to arrive at that moment. They didn't know about all of the missed birthday celebrations, the clothes we hadn't shared, the decades of sisterly advice that hadn't been given. They couldn't fathom the miracle that would manifest in the embrace of siblings who resided on different continents. How could they imagine the impact of our impact? How could I?

The warmth of her hug welcomed me into her heart. It reassured me of our connection and sealed our familial bond for eternity.

Diana asked me if I would like to assist with pre-ceremony preparations. I said yes before she finished her sentence.

I checked each item off the list:

☑ Make reception music playlist suggestions.
☑ Decorate church and reception space.
☑ Pick up floral arrangements.
☑ Attend bride's hair and makeup appointments.
☑ Polish the bride's fingernails.
☑ Style my niece's hair.
☑ Assist with bridal gown on the big day.

Diana's radiant beauty glowed. The floral laced bodice of her custom-made wedding dress covered all the important parts, leaving flesh-toned sheer to take care of the rest. The full skirt's sheer white overlay ruffled at the hem.

I tied the crisscrossed ribbon in the back of her corset as Diana inspected herself in the mirror. I was honored to be the first person to see her in her gown that day.

How different is a German wedding from our American ones? Diana decided to forgo some traditions, like Polterabend. Several days before the church wedding, guests bring old porcelain to break at an informal party. The bridal couple cleans it up together to ward off evil spirits.

German brides wear their engagement ring on the left-hand ring finger. The wedding ring is worn on the right.

A civil ceremony, required by German law, is performed in the town registry office by a justice of the peace. Clergymen are not legally allowed to marry two individuals; however, church rituals often follow the civil ceremony. Some people prefer to do both on the same day. I don't know how they survive. Germans go hard at the reception. They are in it for the long haul.

"I hear receptions in the United States end at midnight." I understood my sister's friend through his thick German accent. He grabbed a seat next to James and me. The DJ kept the dance tunes queued up.

"Most are done by 10:00 p.m.," I said.

I later discovered why he scoffed at our American practices. The DJ's twelve-hour day started to wind down around 4:00 a.m. The amount of American music he played surprised me. Diana even walked down the aisle to "Isn't She Lovely" performed by her wedding singer in English.

Our two-week visit to Europe went by way too fast. Diana messaged me before she left the airport departures drop-off: "Miss u already." I find that goodbyes are the most difficult when it's unclear when the next meeting will be.

In April 2018, I attended our sister Nadine's wedding. In July 2019, Diana's nuptials. For July 2020, our baby sister Devin's big day had been inked on the calendar. Each one began their new chapter in a different age decade, be it their 40's, 30's or 20's, but I'm glad their life milestone took place after I connected with them. Celebrating one of life's grandest moments with each sister was priceless for me.

CHAPTER 15

Wallkill

I SCHEDULED BACK-TO-BACK UPSTATE New York and Illinois trips, beginning in the last few days of July. Airfare rates into New York's Stewart International from Omaha's Eppley Airfield required a sizeable outlay of cash. Months of bargain shopping paid off. I found an affordable ticket.

James parked in the passenger drop-off lane and set my luggage on the walkway. He caressed my hair before his full lips found mine.

"Have a safe trip and tell everyone I said hi. I'll see you next week in Peoria."

"Will do. I love you today." I don't know why we started saying it like that. We've done it for as long as I can remember.

"I love you today," he said. His dimples had grabbed my attention thirty years ago and still gave my tummy butterflies whenever I saw them.

A brilliant idea popped into my head as I approached an Omaha Steaks kiosk on the way to my gate. I couldn't think of a better gift to give my aunt and uncle than world-famous steaks from Omaha.

The salesman showed me a few of the combo pack deals and I settled on one that had four each of top sirloins, steak burgers, boneless chicken breasts, gourmet jumbo franks, and New York cheesecakes. Hopefully, the dessert would measure up to cheesecake served in New York. The kiosk attendant wrapped the box in dry ice and placed it in an insulated cooling bag. He assured me the contents would remain frozen for the duration of my trip. He instructed me to put the bag on the scanner when I went through the security checkpoint. After that, the bag should travel well stowed in my carry-on luggage.

I called Aunt Candy to update her. "Hi, Auntie, my flight gets in at 10:24 p.m."

"Good. I'll pick you up from the airport."

"Thank you, Auntie, that's perfect." My dad's sister and I had communicated via text and phone calls for the past five months. Though I had never seen her in person, I wasn't nervous. Her warm personality put me at ease.

The first leg of my trip went without incident; however, my connecting flight was a bit delayed out of Philadelphia. I landed at Stewart International around 11:30 p.m. I texted my aunt as soon as the flight attendant gave the thumbs up on mobile device usage.

My aunt's son drove his mom's sedan to pick me up. Like my daughter Candace, he was also a junior in college. I hugged the tall track star before he put my luggage in the trunk. My first time meeting a cousin. Ever.

After we greeted each other, Aunt Candy sat on the front passenger side. She turned toward the back seat and handed me a metal water bottle and a reusable bag. It contained two small single-serving bowls, one with diced potatoes and the other with fresh fruit. "Lisa, are you hungry? You must be thirsty; you've been traveling all day."

"So sweet of you to bring me a snack. Thank you."

"You're welcome. It's after midnight and I thought you might want a little something."

I took a few bites of the potatoes and ate all of the apple blueberry mix during the twenty-minute drive to their house.

We turned off the paved road and onto a cul-de-sac, which led to a long driveway on the northwest side of the house. The full moon and motion lights illuminated the acreage surrounding their two-story home.

"Let's get your stuff inside. You'll be staying upstairs in your cousin's room. I had him take his dog since you said you were allergic. He's been staying here for a while, but I didn't want him around bothering you."

"You didn't have to do that, Auntie. I told you, I live with two dogs. I just take my allergy medication, and I'm fine."

"I want you to be comfortable. It's no problem. You're our guest." My aunt set her keys on the table near the door.

I followed my cousin upstairs to his brother's bedroom, which would be my home for the next three days. The large room had two full-size beds next to the wall near the door and an exercise machine close to the windows on the opposite side. I flipped the light switch on and soft music from a boom box filled the room.

I retrieved the Omaha Steaks gift from my luggage and went downstairs.

"Aunt Candy, I brought you something." I handed her the insulated bag.

"What's this?" She read the print on the inside bag and box. "Are these steaks?"

"Yes, there are steaks in there, but also some chicken, hot dogs, and cheesecake." I smiled, pleased with my gift.

"Girl, we're vegan."

"What? Daddy said you used to be, but you weren't anymore."

"I don't know why he told you that. We're all vegan."

"Oh my gosh, Auntie, I am so sorry! I had no idea. I will ship it back home tomorrow."

"No, that's all right, I'll just put it in the freezer."

"If I were you, I wouldn't want that meat in my freezer! Oh my gosh, it's not a problem for me to ship it. They'll pack it in dry ice and it should be fine. I am so sorry, I didn't know, what the heck!"

"No, I'm telling you, Lisa, it's ok. We can give it to my brother-in-law. He's not vegan, he'll love it."

"I feel so bad, are you sure? I am so sorry." My eyebrows crinkled as my hands covered my face. Their meal plan didn't include anything in that box. Not even the cheesecake. FAIL. I texted James, "OMG they are all VEGAN 😑."

When I got back to my bedroom, I noticed a gift bag with an array of colorful triangles printed on it. I picked it up off the nightstand and removed the yellow, pink, and green tissue paper. One by one, I laid the contents out on the bed. Three single-serving packs of California almonds, cashew pomegranate mix, and almond craisin mix. Three packs of personal-size tissues. Toothbrush. Toothpaste. Deodorant. Foot scrubber with brush on the opposite side. Pack of two shower pouf body scrubbers. Full-size bottle of body wash. Microfiber hair wrap. Zebra-patterned sleep mask. Zebra-patterned shower cap. Tiny white battery-operated lamp with colorful dotted plastic shade. The picture of all my gifts was Snapchat Story worthy.

I couldn't wait to thank Aunt Candy. Light from her bedroom let me know she was still awake.

"Auntie, thank you so much for my gift bag. You included everything I need."

"You're welcome, I was happy to do it. Listen, I need to tell you about the shower and show you how to turn it on."

"That's ok, Auntie, I can figure it out. I'll shower in the morning."

"Are you sure you don't want me to show you?"

"Nope, I'm good. Thanks again for my goodies. Good night."

"Good night, dear." Aunt Candy hugged me.

THE SOULFUL SOUNDS OF classic R&B music drifted up the stairs and served as my alarm clock. A note on the bathroom mirror gave me instructions for how to operate the shower.

> Good Morning
> Lisa
>
> In order to
> turn on the
> Shower, Pull the
> Knob of the
> Faucet, it
> will Separate
> and Shower will
> work.
>
> Ex
> Knob ⟶ ⟵ pull down
> P.s. Can't show that

I looked at the shower. I pulled the knob; nothing happened. Was I not pulling it the right way? I tried pulling in the other direction. Nothing. Goodness, I didn't want to break the faucet. Auntie would never invite me back if I damaged her property.

Even with my college degree and thirty years of IT experience, I could not figure out how to turn on the shower. Early in my career, whenever someone asked my family what I did for a living, all they could say was, "She works with computers." Personal computing was new to consumers, but the novelty of it had worn off by the 2010s. Relatives and friends discovered they could consult with me every time they had a question about a mobile phone feature, a computer crash, or a printer jam.

But at that moment, standing in my aunt's bathroom, my technological prowess was rendered worthless. My years of troubleshooting hardware and software problems didn't help me figure out how to operate the shower. I relented after fifteen minutes of trying. I needed help.

"It's a little tricky. Here, pull this down." Aunt Candy demonstrated a gentle two-finger tug on the round part of the faucet stem and initiated the flow of water from the showerhead. Not sure why that was so difficult for me to figure out.

"What's on the agenda for today?" I asked after my shower.

"I like to walk every day. It's good physical therapy for my leg. I'll take you to Chadwick Lake. It's really pretty there."

Mature green trees canopied the dirt trail. A feather appeared in our walkway. I like to believe my mother-in-law, Beatrice, sends them to me from heaven. She was a strong woman who mentored me and loved me as her own.

Nature's melody of summer songs coasted along the gentle breeze. Swimming swans rippled the tranquil water in the distance. I understood why my aunt loved it there.

"We're going to meet my son in the city at 5:00 p.m." She referenced Manhattan with local dialect. "I bought us tickets to a show."

"How far is the city?"

"It takes about an hour and a half on the train. There's one around 2:00 p.m." Aunt Candy guided us in the direction of the parking lot so we could go home and dress for the evening.

Fifteen minutes after leaving the house, we arrived at Beacon Train Station. As we waited for the train to arrive, Aunt Candy applied a nude shade of lipstick to her bottom lip, then smooshed both lips together. A complementary color for her wrinkle-free, cocoa brown, sixty-year-old skin.

"Auntie, why do they call you Candy instead of Gloria?"

"They've called me that since I was a young girl. It's because I'm so sweet!" She smiled wide.

"Since we are going to Manhattan, is there any way we can visit Grandma's apartment?" I was anxious to get my hands on her address book. Daddy said he was unable to find it after she died. He thought it might still be in her condo.

We exited the train at Grand Central Station. I'd been there once before but hadn't taken the time to admire the cathedral-like beauty of the building. I stood under the golden constellations painted on the cerulean blue backdrop of the main concourse ceiling and gazed at the celestial artwork.

We walked through the streets of the city and took in the sights until our footsteps came to a halt in front of Carolines on Broadway, New York City's premier stand-up comedy nightclub.

"Let me call my son and tell him we're here." She took her cell phone out of her purse.

It didn't previously occur to me to ask what show we were going to see. I looked over my left shoulder at the sign: NBC'S MARLON WAYANS July 26–29. Could it be? I asked my aunt if we had tickets to see the famous actor, comedian, screenwriter, and film producer.

"Yeah, I thought this would be a good show. Do you think he's funny?"

"Yes! I used to watch *The Wayans Bros.* on TV all the time. I saw his brother Shawn's routine at a comedy club in Omaha. I'm excited to see Marlon. Thank you for getting us tickets."

"You're welcome. It's 5:00 p.m. now but it looks like we can't enter the club for another hour. I'm getting hungry, are you ready to eat? I packed us some food." I followed Aunt Candy to the patio in front of the comedy club. She arranged a smorgasbord on paper plates in the center of a small red metal table: oatmeal, fruit, and whole wheat sandwiches made with avocado and lettuce.

Three-foot-high planter pots filled with a variety of foliage lined the seating area. A perfect day for a picnic.

Time passed quickly. The club doors opened, allowing natural light to penetrate the dark interior. Auntie and I stopped at the bar before going to our seats. Neither of us consume much alcohol. We ordered virgin versions of our drinks. Strawberry daiquiri for me and piña colada for her. She told me all about some inspirational YouTubers that she followed, and we watched video snippets. Auntie's conversational skills made her quite entertaining. My cousin joined us in the club just as the lights dimmed.

The emcee and the four comedians that took the stage prior to the headliner all made me laugh until I cried. Wil Sylvince, who was of Haitian descent, was our Caribbean neighbor. He commented on how Haitians didn't put an *h* on words like hospital but did put *h*'s on words that didn't need them. Eggs, for example: "I'll take two *h*eggs over *h*easy."

Marlon put a down-to-earth, comedic spin on growing up in a large family, fatherhood, and sibling rivalry with his older brother Shawn.

"Did you enjoy the show?" Aunt Candy led the way out of the club.

"Oh my gosh, yes!" Marlon surprised me with how long he stayed on stage. He spent two hours with us. Aunt Candy got her money's worth.

"I know it's late, but Lisa wanted to go to your apartment," Aunt Candy told her son, checking her watch.

We risked missing the next train. My cousin recommended meeting the next day.

The ride back to Wallkill was filled with girl talk and laughter. I'd never had an aunt so close in age to me. The aunts in my adoptive family were all at least thirty years my senior.

Back in my cousin's room, I opened a small photo album that lay on the nightstand in between the two beds. The 4 x 6 prints told the story of my cousin's high school years, with pictures of school dances and various events.

I stopped on a page with a picture of a little girl sitting in a red chair. Her dark grey corduroy overalls covered a long-sleeve pink shirt. Chin on her hand, her elbow resting on her crossed leg, she smiled for the camera.

I took a picture of it and sent it to my sister with the caption, "Is that you?"

Diana texted a heart eyes emoji. I sent her another picture of her in that same album. Her natural hair had been styled the same, in a curly afro, but her outfit of the day was a white sweater paired with pink and white vertical-striped pants.

"Sooooo cute!!!"

"My five-year old picture." Diana's baby teeth gave it away.

I lay in bed thinking about our trip into the city the next day. If I could get ahold of my mother's address, even if she didn't live there anymore, that would at least be a starting point. Better yet, if I could find one of the letters she wrote to Grandma, I would have a piece of both of them.

BARKING COULD BE HEARD from the other side of the door. My cousin's spunky dog greeted us at the entrance and led us down the hallway, which opened into the living room, which flowed into the dining area. The rectangular kitchen paralleled the entryway.

"Where do you think the address book could be?" Aunt Candy's voice carried down the hallway to her son.

"I don't know. You can check in the closet." He didn't look up from his laptop. He had a work project, and I felt bad for monopolizing his time that afternoon, since we met for lunch prior to walking to his apartment.

"Let's see what we can find." Aunt Candy ruffled through some papers on two of the shelves. She handed me a piece of paper with Daddy's resume on it, before picking up a thin book. "What's this?" She looked at the front and back cover, then gave it to me.

I perused the pages, and while my father's yearbook proved interesting, it contained no clues regarding where my mother once lived.

We further invaded my cousin's privacy and looked through everything in the main hallway closet. No address book. No letters. Even so, I counted that visit as a win, because I stood in the same space where my grandmother once lived, prayed, and took her last breath.

MY UNCLE STOOD IN the kitchen finishing up a snack when we returned home.

"It's so nice to meet you." I walked over to hug him.

"Welcome. I've heard a lot about you."

"Thank you. I appreciate the outpouring of the love from everyone. It was a bit overwhelming at first, but it's been an awesome blessing. I can't even begin to express my gratitude."

"Your story is inspiring to me. I never met my father." My uncle's voice softened.

I didn't know the details surrounding his family history. He didn't go into depth about his situation, but I felt empathy and a connection to him through his words.

"We stopped by the apartment after we had lunch," Aunt Candy said.

"Daddy thought we might find an address for my mother in Grandma Sylvia's book that she kept on her nightstand."

"Did you find the book?" he asked.

"Unfortunately, no." The disappointment in my voice struck a compassionate chord with my uncle.

"Candy, maybe it's in one of those boxes downstairs."

I followed my aunt and uncle into their unfinished basement, hoping the contents of those cardboard boxes and large plastic bags would give clues to solve a five-decade mystery and help lead the way to a reunion with my mother. The desire to reconnect with her grew with a powerful sense of urgency. Time was not on our side and I wanted the opportunity to hug her and see her face in person.

We searched through my grandmother's possessions. Each piece of clothing, every shoe, her pictures and paperwork all helped mold the mental image of my Barbadian ancestor. I didn't find her address book, but I did find *her*.

Nighttime faded into the wee hours of the morning. We kept my uncle up way too late. He needed rest before the start of his Manhattan bus route shift. I thanked him for helping us look through Grandma's things, and he made me promise to keep in touch.

SOULFUL R&B RIFFS SERVED as my alarm clock once again. I had enjoyed myself in Wallkill. We had time for one final excursion before my evening flight.

We parked in the multi-story covered garage at the outdoor mall. Out of the two hundred and twenty premium designer outlet stores and dining establishments, Applebee's was Aunt Candy's restaurant of choice. I welcomed some animal-based protein after my unexpected three-day vegan fast.

"Mom, I'm gonna stop in the Ugg store right quick."

"*Huggs?* Boy, you ain't gettin' no *Huggs*. Them things is $200. That's too expensive!" Oh my—Auntie had done the exact thing the Haitian comedian had said Caribbean people do: put an *h* on a word where it didn't belong.

"I'm not saying I'm going to get anything; I just want to see what they got."

Aunt Candy waved my cousin off as she and I walked toward a clothing store. She sifted through the racks, and when she saw something she liked, she made it work, regardless of the size printed on the tag.

She stepped out of the dressing room wearing white linen pants paired with a white cardigan sweater layered on top of a pale pink shirt.

"Very nice!" I said.

Aunt Candy adjusted the decorative ribbon that criss-crossed down the three-quarter sleeves.

"These pants are so comfortable. They're exactly what I've been looking for."

"You can put your outfit with my stuff, and I'll get it for you." I motioned toward my basket.

"You don't need to do that."

"Auntie, I want to. You bought lunch. This is my treat."

We went back and forth several times until she agreed to let me purchase her ensemble. It was the least I could do to make up for my Omaha Steaks snafu.

We arrived at the airport several hours before my flight.

"You have a bit of time before you have to go through security. Why don't we sit and have a snack?" Auntie brought healthy vegan food with her every time she left the house. I had never before witnessed her level of meal prep and planning. My cousin and I followed her into a small dining area. She removed a reusable lunch bag from her small backpack and set out several glass containers filled with diced potatoes and assorted fruit.

"You're on Snapchat?" My cousin saw me update my Snapchat Story.

"Yep. Me and my girls Snap all the time. Here, do you want to add me?" I positioned my phone toward him with my Snapcode ready for scanning. Soon after, he and I embarked in a candid photo Snapchat war, sending each other pictures we had taken without the other's awareness. Our silliness made both of us laugh until my eyes watered.

"Lisa, I brought you something, take this with you," said Aunt Candy.

"What is it?"

"Ginger root and rosemary. The ginger is good for your stomach." She slid them in front of me.

"I take Dramamine when I fly, and it works great."

"You won't have to take that if you take a bit of this ginger root. It's all you need. Here, I'll put some in this sandwich bag so you can take it with you."

The acrid ginger and rosemary scent permeated through the thin plastic. I feared my purse contents would absorb the odor. I accepted her offering but I made sure the aroma of the all-natural tummy remedy didn't transfer to my belongings.

"It's almost time for me to board my flight. I had so much fun, thank you both for everything. Let's take some pics with my selfie stick before I go."

"You have a selfie stick?" my cousin asked. The sight of it made him laugh. "I've never used one of those before."

"Here, it's simple." I set my phone to camera mode and mounted it on the stick before extending the handle and passing it to him.

"See, easy. Now you've used a selfie stick." I laughed as I removed my phone from the apparatus and collapsed it to fit into my carry-on bag.

Our goodbyes were not tearful, but I wished we didn't live so far apart. Auntie wrapped her arms around me and pressed tightly, ensuring her love would traverse the physical distance that would soon separate us. I walked away with a heart filled with deep affection and gratitude.

CHAPTER 16

Hustled

DADDY'S SMILING FACE WELCOMED me in the airport arrivals waiting area. "I'm happy to see you again. Third time this year!" I walked toward him and offered a hug.

"That's right! How's Candy and family?" Daddy asked.

I told him all about my trip to Wallkill and how I had visited Grandma's apartment but came up short when trying to place my hands on that ever so elusive address book.

"Maybe it'll turn up," Daddy said.

We met Nadine and her children for breakfast the next morning. With impeccable timing, we pulled into the parking lot simultaneously.

"Need help?" We offered Nadine assistance with getting her toddlers out of their car seats.

"Good morning. Could you just keep an eye on my son so he doesn't try to run away?" The quick-footed two-year-old had Grandpa on high alert. The morning sun glistened on my nephew's sandy brown locks as he contemplated whether he should try to run in the parking lot.

The restaurant's bright yellow walls added to the cheery atmosphere of the neighborhood gem. The dining area was to the left, but on our right, a small deli featured homemade eats and an organic market. It was a veritable one stop shop for those looking for groceries and food-related gifts.

The hostess led us to a table with two highchairs. The kids busied themselves with crayons and coloring mats. The menu had both plant- and animal-based options, which made me think it must be one of Nadine's favorite eateries.

Breakfast conversation included talking about dinosaurs and monsters and my niece and nephew demonstrating the noises they made.

"Are you working today?" I asked Nadine.

"Yep. I don't have to be there until noon, so I've got some time. I think there's a park near here. We can take the kids to the playground for a bit." Nadine ruffled my nephew's curls.

I wasn't sure who enjoyed our time the most—the kids, me, or Grandpa. He had not met these grandchildren before the family dinner five months before. They connected a couple of times since then. Another positive post-dinner outcome.

ROB AND I HAD planned to meet later that afternoon. He arrived at my hotel minutes after I did. One of the most valuable things you can give a person is your time. I was grateful for my one-on-one with my brother. I got a scenic tour of the city and surrounding suburbs, while he had to suffer through listening to me sing along to all my favorite pop hits on the radio.

We sat on the patio of a pub, sheltered by a yellow table umbrella that canopied tall wicker back chairs.

"That guy walking this way looks like Anthony."

Rob swiveled in his seat and looked up the sidewalk. "Yep, that's him."

I called out to him when he walked within earshot. "Hey there, brother!"

Anthony's eyes opened wide and his grin matched mine.

"Hey, Sis, what are you doing here?" The surprise and excitement in my little brother's voice warmed my heart.

"I came in a day early for the reunion this weekend."

"What's up, man?" Rob and Anthony shook hands and man hugged.

"Not much, man, I'm just getting off work. I was headed to a bar down the street, but I don't have anything going on," Anthony said.

"Do you want to join us? We're getting ready to have lunch." Rob motioned toward an empty seat at our table.

"I haven't eaten, so yeah, I'll hang out for a bit."

Rain clouds loomed in the distance, but the sun gave us enough natural light for a perfect selfie. The gentle breeze made that eighty-degree afternoon quite pleasant, as did the company of my brothers.

After we had finished eating, Anthony asked, "What are you guys up to next?" He placed his used napkin on his empty plate. Rob and I looked at each other and shrugged.

"We don't have any plans. It's whatever she wants." Rob tilted his head in my direction.

"I have no idea. This is your town. What is there to do?" I asked.

"There's only one thing to do in this city. You know what that is?" Rob said.

I exchanged glances with Anthony before responding, "What's that?"

"Drink," said Rob.

"There's a bar down the street. Do you want to meet my friends?" asked Anthony.

Rob stood and left a few dollars on the table. "Let's do it!"

A downpour of summer rain hit the streets. Good thing I had worn a baseball cap. My curly hair, which I had straightened earlier that morning, would be all too willing to revert to its natural state. I wouldn't mind it so much if the strands of hair grouped together and formed uniform spiral curls. Instead, each strand of my hair prefers to work independently of the others. I use massive amounts of hair product to tame my lion's mane when I wear it natural. I am a Leo, so the look fits, but curly-headed girls know that curls do as curls darn well please.

The neighborhood tavern was three blocks away from the pub where we had dined. Built in 1890, a trap door led to the basement, which housed some dilapidated bowling lanes in much need of remodeling and repair. There was even a secret window that I can't discuss, because, well, then it wouldn't be secret anymore.

Anthony received a greeting like Norm, from the 1980s television show *Cheers,* from his friends when he entered the bar. The handful of people inside welcomed Rob and me with smiles and handshakes.

"Sis, what are you drinking?" Anthony asked.

"I'm not much of a drinker—"

"Hey! What did I say we do in this city?" Rob interrupted.

"Drink." My hypnotic zombie impersonation made my brothers laugh.

"That's right!" Rob was amused at how quickly I had caught on.

"I can tolerate vodka," I said.

"Cool, how do you like it?" Anthony asked.

"I don't know, I told you I'm not a drinker!"

"Maybe you'd like a Slutty Temple," said Rob.

"What the heck is that?" I asked.

"Vodka, 7up, and grenadine." Rob's former bartending knowledge came in clutch.

"I can probably handle that. Light on the vodka, please."

"Do you know how to play pool?" Anthony motioned toward the pool table.

"My husband bought a brand-new pool table three years ago, and I've never played on it. Our last name is embroidered in the felt." My brothers teased me about being fancy.

"You up for cutthroat?" Anthony said to Rob.

"Yeah, that's cool. Lisa, you in?" Rob asked me.

"I have no idea what that is. Do I have to call my pocket? My balls tend to go in anywhere," I said.

"Each person has a set of five balls: one through five, six through ten, and eleven through fifteen," Rob explained.

"Oooh, I like stripes!" I said with excited-little-girl glee. I suffered from Asian flush, and my first few sips of Slutty Temple had started to kick in.

"You'll have to knock in one of the lower balls. Then you get to choose your set," said Anthony.

"Huh?" I needed more instruction.

"The object of the game is to knock everyone else's balls in and leave yours on the table. The first person to knock in a ball gets to choose their set," Rob explained.

"Ah, ok, I got it."

The sound of ice clinking in our drinks accompanied us to the table. Cues hung in racks on the wall. My brothers let me take the first shot to break the balls. I chalked up the tip of my stick and managed to drop a low number ball into a pocket.

"I want eleven through fifteen." I got my stripes.

Modeling after the professional pool player Black Widow, my next three shots sank my brothers' pool balls into hole after hole after hole. They both looked at each other, then at me. I couldn't do anything except laugh.

"Man, we just got straight hustled!" Rob's hands went up in the air as he looked at Anthony in disbelief.

"No, seriously, I haven't played in years!" I had no idea how I made all those shots in a row, especially since I had to specify which pocket I intended the ball to go into. Even the Black Widow would have been low-key impressed.

"Uh huh. Yeah, right!" Anthony said as he shook his head.

"I like the little stripey ones," Rob mocked as he walked around the table. "Man...hustled." He laughed.

They told me a few stories of times when they had been

hustled or when they had done the hustling. I had no idea that was a thing.

A few games and drinks later, we said our goodbyes to Anthony. Rob and I were off to our next stop.

We walked around the riverfront and talked about our lives, interests, and families.

"My wife and I went to this concert down here, and it was a band she really loves. One of the band members looked at her, and she just lost it. I mean, she ugly cried, she was so excited."

"Who would you ugly cry over?" I asked Rob.

"First of all, it's impossible for me to ugly cry," Rob said.

"Oh, my bad. If it were somehow possible—it's not, since you're so handsome and all—but if you could ugly cry, who would it be over?"

"Good question. I don't think anyone. Who would *you* ugly cry over?" Rob asked me.

"Prince. I saw him in concert three times, but never got to meet him. He would make me ugly cry. If you could have dinner with anyone, who would it be with?" I asked.

"Do they have to be alive or can they be dead?"

"Either."

Rob pondered my question. "My grandmother." He looked at the ground as he walked.

I almost stepped on a white feather. I held it up to get a good look at it. The downtown skyline started to shadow in front of the setting sun.

"Don't pick that up, you know it's got bird syphilis on it," Rob said. I playfully punched him in the arm.

"It does not! My mother-in-law sends me these. Maybe your grandma is with you now. Which grandma?"

"My mom's mom. I was pretty close to her."

We continued walking and talking and stopped into a trendy bar. I placed my feather in a planter near the entrance, then made a beeline to the restroom as Rob ordered drinks for us. Seated on the patio, Rob took a deep drag of a cigarette and released a puff of smoke into the air.

"So do you have any regrets?" I asked my brother.

"No, I don't have a lot." He flicked some ashes into a tray. "Maybe the only thing I do regret is losing a pin I got from Anthony. When I was a kid, one of the few times I was over to our dad's house, Anthony walked in. He wore a black leather jacket. He had a pin on it, and I thought it was cool. He gave it to me. I had it for several years, until I lost it. Man, I was pissed. If I could get that back, that'd be cool." Rob took another drag of his cigarette.

How different would our lives have been if all my siblings and I had been raised together? What type of bond would we have? I know it's a moot point. What matters now is the type of bond we have moving forward.

I picked my feather out of the planter, and we headed back toward the car.

"I had a lot of fun today. Thank you so much for rearranging your schedule to hang out with me. I really appreciate it," I said.

"It's not often we get to hang out. It was no problem." We hugged goodbye and I walked toward the hotel entrance.

"Hey, Lisa!"

I turned around.

"The door is that way." He laughed as he pointed in the opposite direction.

"Yes. Yes, it is. Good night, Rob! Thanks!"

I had to laugh at myself. All the years of teasing, giving each other a hard time, getting under each other's skin, sibling rivalry, competition, inside jokes, sharing, caring, advising, listening, loving, and existing in the same space, were all experiences that I missed out on with my siblings. My brother and I got a good start on making up for lost time.

CHAPTER 17

Motherland

ONE MONTH BEFORE MY Korea trip, I tapped into Daddy's memory bank for reconnaissance.

"Do you remember where the photographer was located in the village?" I zoomed in on the satellite view of the map. Daddy repositioned my iPad to get a better look.

"It was five businesses in off the main road from Munsan-ni. This looks much different. There were no paved roads or cars when I was there. According to this, they have a gas station and a school now." Daddy studied the aerial view of the village.

"Do you know how old Ahjussi was when you were there?"

"He was around thirty."

I had pictured a much older man but welcomed that news. He could still be living in the same neighborhood. Koreans tended to have long life lines and it wasn't uncommon for elders to live beyond their one hundredth birthday.

"Do you remember where Ahjussi lived in relation to the photography studio?"

"Go two more businesses down and hang a right at the alleyway. That led to her uncle's place." His photographic memory astounded me.

"Daddy, if you knew exactly where we were, why didn't you ever come back to try to find us?" I searched my father's eyes for the answer. The windows to his brown irises were boarded up, keeping the truth in darkness. He stared blankly at me.

"I didn't have the means."

My eyebrows crinkled. "What are you saying?"

"I was in the military. I wasn't allowed to go back to Korea. I would have had to get permission from a commanding officer, and they weren't going to let me do that."

"You were in the military for less than ten years. You've been a civilian for over forty years now." I sat up straight in my chair.

"I didn't have the wherewithal."

I paused to contemplate what he had said. It didn't make sense to me. His response made me think my question caught him off guard.

"I don't believe you." I shook my head. "You told me you earned $6,000 per month while working in Germany. Anthony and I are seventeen months apart, and nine of those months are gestational. Daddy, you moved on. It never crossed your mind to come back for my mother or me."

"What do you want me to say?"

"I don't know. You once told me you wanted to have a lot of kids, and you did. But you didn't help raise them. You left that up to their mothers. But you had to know the Korean society would have made that difficult for my mother to raise a mixed-race child. You didn't even try to help us."

The realization of my words opened a deep wound that I hadn't known existed. The trauma of abandonment didn't surface for me until that moment, and the pain was devastating. I couldn't let it go.

"You live in the same city as three of your children, yet you didn't spend Father's Day with any of them. I think that's pretty sad. You didn't raise my brothers and sisters as siblings. Maybe their moms made that difficult. Perhaps there's some

Caribbean cultural difference. I don't know." I raised my hands in exasperation.

Daddy looked at me. He had heard enough of what I had to say.

"What do you want to hear? That I thought you were dead? Or that your mother threw you away?"

His words, hardened by sarcasm, ravaged my heart until it was unrecognizable. It was such an insensitive thing to say to an adoptee. He made me feel as if I were no better than unwanted trash.

I stood up, grabbed some clean clothes out of my suitcase, and rushed to the bathroom, leaving him sitting alone in the spare bedroom.

My flood of tears intermingled with the water droplets in the shower sanctuary. I cried in there for almost an hour. Every time I tried to pull myself together, the sting from what he said slapped me. But I didn't want him to see me cry. I didn't want him to know how hurt or damaged I was.

I needed to get home. I left his house at 4:00 p.m. to drive back to Omaha. Six hours later I pulled into my driveway. I melted into James's arms as we laid in bed. I told him what Daddy had said to me and how it made me feel. James didn't respond. He looked at me and was listening, but he said nothing. My unwillingness to tolerate the five-minute silence led me to find solace in a shower sanctuary for the second time in twelve hours. This time, the only moisture hitting my cheeks was the droplets emanating from the square shower head. I'd left all my tears on Interstate 80 on the drive home.

Anger replaced the hurt feelings from the afternoon. Ire with myself for thinking non-adoptees should somehow understand how it feels to be abandoned, unwanted, lost, or thrown away, whether by choice or circumstance. It's a very unrealistic thought process. How could anyone who had never been in the same situation grasp the pain of chronic loss that adoptees carry within their hearts? How could they relate to the mental anguish and hopelessness associated with trying to locate birth parents, who hold the keys to our identity, when we have very little clues to their whereabouts? Someone who's never experienced that type of persistent grief shouldn't be expected to comprehend the relentless pain.

MY SEAT FROM DALLAS to Incheon International Airport had no power. That left me with no use of in-flight entertainment or electrical charging on the thirteen-hour flight to Seoul. I hoped the airline would offer me a free upgrade when I returned home in two weeks. The flight attendant could only authorize a three-thousand-mile credit to my frequent flier account. She recommended I check with a gate agent after the plane landed, but finding my hosts became my main priority after arrival.

Twelve adoptees from across the globe participated in G.O.A.'L's First Trip Home program in August 2019: six from the United States and six from Europe. Staff members met us after we arrived at the airport and escorted each participant, via public transportation, to our hostel.

No memories of my mother or Korea remained in my consciousness. Fifty years had passed by. I'm glad I waited until adulthood before returning to my homeland. I savored every moment—good and bad. I nodded at the *Welcome to Korea* sign above the doorway as I exited the jet bridge. I paused before stepping onto Korean soil. The last time I was there was the year the world-famous Beatles band broke up and Richard Nixon was president of the United States. Bustling city traffic whirled around me as I took a deep breath of polluted air and marveled at the tall buildings that crowded the Seoul skyline. I'd never been so fully immersed in an environment so different from American culture. It was fascinating and overwhelming all at the same time.

Ghastly pale women wore peach eyeshadow above and below their lash line, pairing it with an orangish-red lip color. Conversations with the locals revealed the desire to look more Western as the driving force behind the glamour standard. South Koreans led the world in the male beauty market. I stepped into an ecosystem where heterosexual young men wore foundation, lipstick, and eyebrow enhancements. Those same men also had no qualms about holding hands with each other in public, something that is uncommon amongst heterosexual men in the US.

Low ceilings and sinks made me wonder how a man of James's height would fare in this country. Handwashing required my 5'4" body to bend ninety degrees to reach the sink in public restrooms. Soap on a stick, protruding from the wall, replaced liquid soap. If there was soap at all.

I couldn't see myself living in a place where the sewer system and poor water pressure forbade flushing toilet paper. My affinity for that practice surfaced once I could no longer do it. Squat toilets scared me, so I steered clear. I peeked at the holes in the floor from a distance, afraid of getting too close. Some had porcelain hoods, others were grate covered. How did one prevent urine splatter and soiled clothes? Good thing our hosts had warned us about the lack of toilet paper in some bathrooms. I made sure to locate supply before I used the facilities, sometimes finding it hanging on a wall outside of the stall or in vending machines near the restroom entrance.

Koreans preferred to use toilet paper squares as napkins. Imagine my surprise to find a commercial-sized roll mounted on a column in the middle of a restaurant dining room, instead of in a bathroom where I expected to see it.

Wooden chopsticks in the US never posed a problem for me, but the metal variety in Korea took some getting used to. Lotioned hands combined with summer's humidity made them difficult to keep in my hands. I'm sure my face turned red when a restaurant worker brought me a fork. That first meal in Korea also taught me that to-go bags were not customary. Most restaurants were not equipped to package leftovers unless they offered delivery service.

I also had to get used to communal meals. Banchan, small side dishes, accompanied every meal and were meant to be shared by table guests. My inner germophobe ignored everyone else's chopsticks as they picked bite-sized morsels from the small plates.

Another thing I ignored were the fish heads floating in our soup. Korean custom reserved them for the oldest in the group, which was me. No thank you, I'll pass. We didn't follow the custom of waiting for the oldest to start eating before everyone else helped themselves. We all dug in together.

We did find it fun to have the youngest in the group pour the first round of soju shots. Korean custom forbids that person from pouring their own, and they must turn away from the group to drink it, otherwise it is considered rude.

Thankfully, the guest house where we lodged provided Western beds instead of traditional sleeping mats. What they didn't provide were sheets. Bedding consisted of a white mattress pad and thin yellow quilt that barely covered the top of the mattress.

Shower shoes lay at the entrance of the bathroom. I found it odd that a showerhead mounted on the wall in between the toilet and the sink was barrier and partition free. It got everything in the bathroom wet, including towel racks, the toilet seat, and the back of the sink. Somehow, the toilet paper stayed dry. Koreans used hand towels, instead of bath towels, for drying bodies and hair.

Public transportation made it easy to travel around the city, but coffee drinkers beware. City bus drivers exercised their legal right to refuse boarding to passengers who had not finished their cup of java. Good luck finding a public trash can to toss your cup. The government had banned them due to stringent recycling rules.

Our group discovered that talking amongst ourselves on the city bus was deemed offensive. "Be quiet! Be quiet!" A local woman scolded us in English. She glared and pointed at each of us before exiting at the next stop.

I'd learned to navigate the subway system by the end of my two-week stay—standing room only, shoulder to shoulder. Naver search engine replaced the nonfunctional Google Maps. And ladies, no smoking while walking in public. It's illegal to do so. Not sure why it's ok for men, though.

Overstimulation became difficult to avoid. Heavy traffic, businesses, shops, restaurants, pedestrian overcrowding, and an overabundance of signs occupied every square inch of Hongdae, the trendy district surrounding Hongik University.

MY GROUP STARTED OUR birth family search at the Seoul Seodaemun Police Station. Detectives collected our DNA samples so we could be included in the National Missing Children's database. Not all adoptees were relinquished. Some kids were found roaming the streets or were inadvertently separated from their families. People who found stray children often took them to organizations that facilitated adoptions. Having our DNA in that database would help if Korean family members initiated a search, which some do.

Our next stop was the Jumin community center to get a copy of our family register. Those fortunate enough to have the name of a parent received additional information that could possibly aid in their search. Daddy knew my mother as Chung Suk-ah, but my adoption paperwork had her name listed as Lee, Ok Soon. She could have given a false name to both. I hoped I would know by the end of my trip.

The National Center for the Rights of the Child (NCRC) is a Korean government agency that helps with birth family searches. All paper copies of child records from defunct orphanages and baby homes are stored in NCRC's archive facility. During a trip to their office, we were shown a presentation of their services and how they assist adoptees.

Day three for me included a visit to Holt Korea, the agency that had facilitated my adoption. A case worker reviewed my file but gave me no new information. She had an address for my mother, but due to privacy laws she would not give it to me. Koreans protect the privacy of birth mothers while denying adoptees their right to know about key parts of their lives. They have information about us that they refuse to share. Some records are incomplete, missing, or falsified. It appears they never expected us to come back and demand the details.

Day four's excursion took me to the Ilsan Orphanage. I stood in the middle of the traffic-free road on the sprawling campus. I stretched both arms out to the side and looked up toward the sky. Five decades prior, I had walked that same road as a toddler. My mother brought me to that facility on July 11, 1969, one month shy of my second birthday. That's the last place where I saw my umma. I walked onto the grounds with her, and she walked off without me.

The original buildings were gone, but pictures of them hung in Holt Memorial Hall. A special needs school became the campus focal point, servicing community members as well as orphanage residents.

Harry and Bertha Holt started Korean adoptions in 1955 by bringing eight war orphans into their family, thus opening the door for other families to follow suit beginning in 1956. The Holt orphanage mandated that all mixed-race kids must be adopted internationally. Harry understood the challenges we would face if we remained in Korea.

The Holts were trailblazers who navigated uncharted territory. Their actions affected generations worldwide. My visit that day included an impromptu stop at their daughter's house, located within the grounds. Molly had worked tirelessly alongside her parents, helping special needs orphans. I had read interviews online given by her and her biological siblings, and they revealed they believed helping Korea's homeless children was a calling God placed in their lives.

Molly passed away in the spring of 2019, three months before my trip. I walked up the steep brick stairway to view her headstone. She had been laid to rest next to her parents, in a burial site that overlooked the Ilsan Center campus.

Staff physician Dr. Cho resided in Molly's home. She'd worked at the orphanage since 1961. She provided care to me during my measles episode in 1969. She welcomed me into her home and spoke of the history of their work.

I looked through photo albums, categorized by month and year. The Holt's legacy came alive on those pages. The pictorial view of life at the orphanage didn't spark any memories but did make me more appreciative for the care I was provided while I was a resident.

Day five of my journey took me to my birthplace, two hours north of Seoul, close to the DMZ. I had difficulty locating the countryside village on Google Maps before I left the United States. I figured out that the spelling had changed from Nul No Ri to Neullori. I had lived there with my mother for a couple of years, but none of it felt familiar.

My G.O.A.'L birth family search mentor printed flyers with my story and picture. She arranged for a young Korean translator from Seoul to accompany me and recommended we hand them out to anyone we spoke with and post them within the village.

My translator was in his early twenties and very eager to help me with my search. The first person we encountered was a real estate agent who had lived in the tiny village since 1958. We stood in his office while he studied the flyer and looked at the pictures we brought of my umma and Daddy. The realtor looked at me, then back at the pictures. The translator asked him if he knew my mom, but he didn't answer right away. He read every word of the flyer.

"Why didn't she get the information from the adoption agency?" His response, in Korean, seemed angry. He read through each word of the flyer again. He glared at me, his face stern with callous indifference.

"Show him the picture of my mom and me standing in front of her house. Ask him if he knows where that house is." I motioned toward one of the photos laid out on a small table between myself and the older gentleman.

"He just keeps saying the agency should have told you about your mom. I said that's all the information we have." The translator pointed to the flyer, which the older gentleman read—again.

"My dad said they befriended a photographer in the village. Those pictures of the two of them were taken at his studio. Ask him if he knows where that studio was, or if the photographer is still here."

"Those women who opened their doors for the soldiers and laid down with them never used their real name." The man stared at me with disapproval as he spoke in my native tongue. I couldn't understand his words as he said them, but I understood his demeanor.

"What did he say about the photographer?" I asked.

"He said they didn't have cameras back then."

I looked at the translator in disbelief. Spread out on the table in front of the old man were photos, apparently taken by a camera that didn't exist. He had more information than he was willing to give me. There were only about sixty residences in the entire village, and I was certain he knew every building and everybody who lived there.

We walked down the street to a nursing home. A young woman greeted us in the lobby and asked us to wait while she found someone to answer our questions. Two men appeared and the translator showed them the picture of my umma and Daddy. One of the men laughed and walked away. The other man said he didn't know a Chung Suk-ah or Lee, Ok Soon.

We walked back to the main road and looked down the street to determine our next steps.

"We need to go back to the nursing home and ask that guy if there's a doctor or dental office in town. I would think at some point within the last fifty years she would have had to get some type of medical attention. Maybe if they don't recognize my umma, they might recognize the lady in the background of one of those pictures. This town is so small, someone's got to know something."

The gentleman we had spoken to moments earlier met us at the entrance. He had checked his resident registry for the names we gave. The search returned two matches, but only on the name and not the birthdate. Both of those residents were deceased. The nearest doctor was a few towns away, and the village did not have a dental office.

The sun beamed high in the sky, making beads of sweat form on my brow. We walked along the main road, stopping to tape my flyers to bus stop shelters and pedestrian bridges. I was on a missing person poster. It made my heart sad to look at them...to look at me.

Meager housing in the village starkly contrasted the thirty-story high-rise apartment buildings sprinkled throughout South Korea's most populated districts. Those spectacular residential clusters rivaled the horizons of major metropolitan areas in the US. But the one-story homes in this rural neighborhood were run-down shacks made of brick, cinder block, or corrugated tin. Thatched roofs from the 1960s had been replaced by that same corrugated tin in shades of blue, gray, or burgundy.

We walked the housing development three times, searching for my umma's cinder block house. We couldn't make a positive match to the one in my picture. Paved roads covered the dirt pathways my toddler feet had once walked upon. Chili peppers lay drying in the yards of the residents. Pet dogs walked to the end of their chains to greet us. Good thing they were leashed. I was afraid of every dog except my own, especially big dogs.

Most of the townspeople remained inside, sheltered from the sweltering afternoon heat. My interpreter and I planned to speak with any older residents we encountered, ones who may have been around in 1967.

"Excuse me, do you know this woman? This is her daughter and she is looking for her mother." The interpreter approached a woman pulling weeds from her garden. She walked to the edge of her fenced-in yard and told the interpreter she did not know my umma and that I should stop looking. She said I was wasting my time trying to find her and that she was probably dead.

We walked until we spotted another woman exiting her house. "Does this woman look familiar? Her daughter was adopted and would like to find her."

The woman examined the picture of my umma and Daddy, then spoke directly to me in Korean. "How the fuck am I supposed to know her when she's married to that n*gger? No one was adopted from here. Stop trying."

The interpreter, taken aback by her racist remarks, withdrew the pictures, and we continued our hunt for people who might give us clues as to my umma's whereabouts.

"You have to stop showing people the picture of my parents. It makes them too hostile. I have no idea what they're saying, but I can read body language, the tone of their voice, and the way they look at me. I know it's not good."

"I thought those pictures were going to be the ones to jar their memories. They should remember a black guy in the neighborhood." The interpreter kicked a rock in the road.

"Trust me, they remember." I shook my head. He had never encountered that level of racism in his young life, but I was no stranger to it. Living as a minority in the United States was all I knew. It was no surprise to me that my minority status also stood out in my motherland, amongst the sea of pale

Asian faces that didn't match my hapa (half) Korean complexion. I'd expected it.

"Let's go down this road. I think we may have missed this one," I said.

Two steps in, a dog popped out of a cage, barking in our direction. Chains prevented him from darting toward us. We took one more step and another dog jetted out of a neighboring cage. Their snarling signaled eight other dogs on both sides of the road to exit cages and test the strength of their restraints.

"Abort, abort!" I grabbed the interpreter's arm and we ran in the opposite direction until the dogs and their barking were no longer a threat.

"Man, that was weird! I wonder why they had so many dogs?" I said. I'd never seen anyone with that many pets.

Our breathing returned to normal as we continued walking down a street we had already traversed. I pointed out a woman with a walker taking tiny steps down a slight incline. She looked to be in the same generation as my mother.

"We are looking for this woman. Do you know who she is?" The elderly lady barely glanced at the picture of my umma and Daddy. "No," was all she said, and she kept walking, passing by me without establishing eye contact.

"That's probably her." I chuckled.

"You think so?"

"Look at my mom's face. That lady's a little bit heavier and fifty years older. That could have definitely been her." We laughed at the thought, but I was only half-joking.

"We're getting nowhere with you showing the pictures with Daddy in them. Just show people the one of my umma standing in front of the tree, or the one where she's holding me in front of the house."

The interpreter relented. "My mind is blown by how vicious they are. All the racial slurs and cuss words...what's wrong with these people? It's like they are stuck in the 1950s."

I couldn't even get emotional about it. It wasn't the first time I'd experienced racism and it wouldn't be the last. That's just part of me living in my skin. I'm not able to take my Koreanness and Blackness off and lay them to the side, nor would I ever want to. I don't take them off when I go to bed at night. I go to sleep with them, I wake up with them, and I proudly wear them all day long.

We entered a small convenience store to find respite from the heat and humidity. I paid for our drinks as the interpreter spoke with the cashier.

"We're looking for this woman. Her name is Chung Suk-ah or Lee, Ok Soon. Do you know her?" The interpreter handed the older man the picture of my umma posing in front of a large tree.

He adjusted his glasses. "That tree used to be near the bridge as you come into town. It's not there anymore. All of the big trees were cut down years ago." We knew of the bridge he referenced. I had taped my missing person poster there. He was the nicest person we spoke to in the entire village.

Our focus on finding my umma caused us to miss lunch. I looked at my watch. 3:10 p.m. "I'm starting to get hungry. I saw some restaurants on the main road. Let's try the one where we saw that lady sweeping earlier," I said.

We opened the door and found the woman near the back of the dining area, sleeping on a mat. We startled her as we entered. We hadn't known that Neullori shut down at 3:00 p.m. for naptime. My 6:00 a.m. breakfast had worn off four hours ago. We walked down the street and stopped in the parking lot of another restaurant.

"Oh my god, they serve dog meat!" The interpreter put his hand to his head.

"How do you know?"

"Because it says it on the sign." He pointed to the Korean writing on the building.

"Nooo! Wait…do you think those dogs we saw earlier—"

"Yep, probably so. I've heard of dog farms but never saw one until today," he said.

A mental image of those poor puppies materialized. Two million dogs per year were sold for fighting and food. The Seoul city government banned dishes such as earthworm soup and dog stew during the 1988 Olympics, but according to national news sources, back alleys and rural areas didn't comply with those guidelines.

"Ok—I'm done! Let's get out of here," I said.

I left the angst that had fueled my search in the hills and chili pepper farms that surrounded Neullori. Village residents had no compassion and no incentive to help me find my umma. They treated me like an ugly blemish on their homogenous society. I was a living reminder of a savage war.

The key piece of information I walked away with that day was that I didn't know my mother's name nor her birthdate. Back to square one.

I spent the rest of my time in Korea as a tourist, visiting beaches, fish markets, museums, Buddhist temples, and bustling entertainment and shopping districts. I didn't find my umma, but I intimately experienced a culture that should have been familiar but, instead, was foreign to me.

I bonded with my fellow adoptees during the grueling active birth search process. We leaned on each other throughout our journey. My new friends told me they saw beauty in me, even though the Korean society looked at my dark skin with disdain. When emotions overflowed, we cried together and encouraged one another. We celebrated each other's reunions, family discoveries and victories, no matter how miniscule or magnificent.

Our last First Trip Home group session gave us vital tips for mentally processing our experience. Counselors gave all participants recommendations for communicating about our journey to relatives and friends once we returned home. They told us it was ok to tell as much or as little about the trip as we wanted and asking for space and time to sort out our feelings was normal and encouraged. It's typical for people who knew we were going to Korea to ask how the trip went, but it was also acceptable for us to tell them if we weren't ready to discuss the details.

One-third of the participants reunited with their biological mothers, fathers, and/or siblings during those two weeks. One-third obtained additional information that may aid their search. The final third left that peninsula with more questions than answers. I was one of the latter.

Our family and friends back home would have no idea how life altering that trip had been. We were expected to meld back into our lives as if we were unchanged by our journey.

CHAPTER 18

DNA

NICK AND DEVIN'S MOM was no longer married to our dad, but it was cool that we were all invited to her family reunion. Other close friends who had become family also took part in the weekend's festivities, where there was an abundance of food, fun, and laughs. Capris and Candace had no problems socializing with cousins who were close to their age. We weren't amongst strangers, even though we had just met the majority of the people present that day.

The August sun elevated the 10:00 a.m. temperature to eighty-five degrees, a precursor to the sweltering day that lay ahead at the Illinois State Fair. Nick and Devin's brother was my seat partner on the bus ride.

"Lisa, you don't know how much you've done for this family," he said.

"Really? What do you mean?"

"You have found a way to bring us together. On your first trip, when you got all the siblings together for dinner…that had never happened before. And you hanging out with Anthony and Rob, and Nadine and her family—stuff like that just hasn't happened in the past." I appreciated his candor. The picture of the family dynamic was becoming clearer.

"Nick said he's still trying to figure out how the dinner happened," I said. "I'm just so thankful everyone is open to it. And how they've embraced me and my family...I can't even tell you how much that means to us."

"I understand how you feel. Not knowing your family for all those years. I've never met my father," he said.

"I didn't realize that."

"High school relationship, didn't work out between my mom and him. But your dad was a father figure to me during my teenage years. I've always gotten along well with him. He's a good dude. Thank you for being a light unto our family. Whenever you come in town, everyone is all excited. 'Lisa's coming.' 'Lisa's gonna be here.' It's been great."

His gratitude humbled me, but I knew none of that was my doing. I'm happy God had used me as a vehicle to aid our family in reconnecting.

The weather forecast correctly predicted the summer heat wave that engulfed the state fair ground. Our powder blue t-shirts were drenched with sweat by the time 2:00 p.m. rolled around. I was ready for a reprieve and a cool shower.

Our entertainment during the evening family chill time was an original rap from DNA (Devin, Nick, and Anna-Marie).

♫*DNA in your blood stream*♫

Nick:
Yeah, ay, I'm paleo I don't need the beat I just eat the snare
My famo say they on they way and I'm already there
(Hey guys)
They got the drank, that mac and cheese, and all the shirts they wear on
And I can promise you one thing, Stan ain't got that air on
(Man, we hot!)
You finna sweat, you finna laugh, you finna eat it up
We do the track like it's some leftovers and heat it up
(microwave sounds)
Now call your momma if you're scared cuz we about to party
Hit 414 ignition switches, then we get it started!

Devin:
Um, I be where the family be, I paid my hundred-dollar fee,
so I can get this family tee
You see me hang with Uncle D? I'm tryna learn that history
Fam so big found new members on Ancestry
It's very unlikely I miss this time with family
Flying in from every coast, can't wait for who I'm 'bout to
see
Lookin' at the menu, let's see what we about to eat
Havin subs on Thursday, run me that ham and cheese
Movin' on to Friday, can't wait to get that ghetti
(Niece Olivia: Some please)
Barbecue on Saturday, boy, you know I'm ready, yeh
(Niece Olivia: I'm ready)

Anna-Marie:
You got Devin, Nicholas, and Anna-Marie
Using just our letters, we got DNA
Same stuff that you find in your family blood
When we get together we give a hug, a handshake, a dap, or
even a kiss
Seeing all the people that you oh so miss
So who's new that we have this time around
Another baby—What? That isn't profound
We've added another almost every year
We've got new friends and siblings also here
Turning up and celebrating each other's what we do
Ever need help, you know we got you
Graduated last month from massage therapy
Had three kids and was in my fourth pregnancy
Still no better time for me to be inspired
Ask me how I am? That's easy. I'm tired.
(Niece Alexandria: Wake up!)
Welcome, come in, get ready to eat
Being part of this family is oh so sweet
(Nephew Gideon: I love youuu)

Outro:
Nick: Check it yo
Anna-Marie: We're not rappers
Nick: We are not rappers

Devin: DNA
Nick: D N A

Cheers erupted as the song finished. Great-grandfather's entertainer gene thrived.

I looked around at my family and new friends who had become family. I had enjoyed getting to know each one on different levels. The laughter. The family bond. I inhaled a deep breath of appreciation for the inclusive, welcoming, accepting, and loving spirit that filled the room.

I loved the way Anna-Marie flew my infant nephew around like an airplane, landing at everyone in the room for a good night kiss. Each person searched for a spot on his head or face that hadn't been kissed already.

I loved Devin's dance moves.

I loved the way my nieces and nephew ended our FaceTime calls saying "Te quiero, Tia!" in unison.

I loved the way Rob made spending time with me a priority, and how his wife reached out to me when her work brought her to Omaha.

I loved how Nadine and I shared what was going on in our lives, even though it sometimes took her several days to respond to a message.

I loved Anthony's reaction when I called him "little brother." He laughed and said, "No one has ever said that to me before!"

I loved how Diana agreed to do the Daniel Fast with Capris and me. She prayed for me to find my mom. I prayed for her to have a baby since she had been trying for years. She and her husband welcomed a baby boy in February 2020.

I loved the way Nick had January 16 marked on his calendar as Li Sibling Anniversary, because he said that's the day I stormed into his life.

DNA. DNA is not only a game changer, it's a *life* changer.

Epilogue

The Korean government has made an effort to help its 167,000 international adoptees by funding organizations and programs that provide services such as birth family search and language education scholarships. Law makers have passed legislation that allows adoptees to be eligible for F-4 Overseas Korean Visas, which gives adoptees access to national health care and the right to live and work in Korea for three year periods. During the COVID-19 worldwide pandemic, the Korean government was instrumental in supplying free face masks to adoptees residing across the globe.

Living a productive life with the wonderful people God surrounded me with doesn't suppress my desire to have jeong—the Korean concept of warm feelings and attachment shared in a close relationship—with my Korean umma.

But sometimes, when we ask, God tells us no. Think of it this way. A young child asks her father if she can play in the street. He knows the dangers associated with her request, and tells her no. Instead, he offers to take her to a park, where she can play without worrying about getting hit by a car. Our Heavenly Father protects us in that same way. He knows the dangers associated with our requests, and sometimes choses to shield us, and protect us from ourselves. I'm still in that park.

My DNA is in a multitude of databases now. The Lord will decide when I will connect with someone on my maternal side, be it a sibling, cousin, or even my mother herself. Judging from the Christmas card my umma sent Daddy, she and I believe in the same God. I understand that the inner peace I seek may not materialize until my umma and I are reunited in eternity.

About the Author

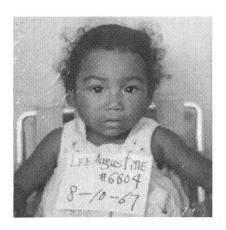

Lisa A. Quaites is an IT professional by trade but discovering her biological family via DNA testing prompted her to pen her debut memoir, *Faith & Favor*. The search for her Korean mother put her on the path to find her Barbadian father, and her life has been forever changed. Lisa and her husband James call Omaha, Nebraska, home. She has a stepson, Chris, and two daughters, Capris (the *i* sounds like a long *e* and the *s* is silent) and Candace.

Made in the USA
Columbia, SC
08 January 2021